GIS

Bloomsbury Research Methods

Edited by Graham Crow and Mark Elliot

The Bloomsbury Research Methods series provides authoritative introductions to a range of frequently used research methods and of current issues in research methodology. Each volume sets out the key elements of the particular method and features examples of its application, drawing on a consistent structure across the whole series. Written in an accessible style by leading experts in the field, this series is an innovative pedagogical and research resource.

What are Community Studies?
Graham Crow

What is Diary Method?
Ruth Bartlett and Christine Milligan

What is Discourse Analysis?
Stephanie Taylor

What is Grounded Theory?
Massimiliano Tarozzi

What is Inclusive Research?
Melanie Nind

What is Narrative Research?
Molly Andrews, Mark Davis, Cigdem Esin, Lar-Christer Hyden, Margareta Hyden, Corinne Squire and Barbara Harrison

What is Online Research?
Tristram Hooley, Jane Wellens and John Marriott

What is Qualitative Interviewing?
Rosalind Edwards and Janet Holland

What is Qualitative Research?
Martyn Hammersley

What are Qualitative Research Ethics?
Rose Wiles

What is Social Network Analysis?
John Scott

What is Qualitative Longitudinal Research?
Bren Neale

What is Rhythmanalysis?
Dawn Lyon

Forthcoming books:

Embodied Inquiry
Jennifer Leigh and Mag Nicole Brown

Statistical Modelling in R
Kevin Ralston, Vernon Gayle, Roxanne Connelly and Chris Playford

GIS

Research Methods

Nick Bearman

BLOOMSBURY ACADEMIC
LONDON • NEW YORK • OXFORD • NEW DELHI • SYDNEY

BLOOMSBURY ACADEMIC
Bloomsbury Publishing Plc
50 Bedford Square, London, WC1B 3DP, UK
1385 Broadway, New York, NY 10018, USA

BLOOMSBURY, BLOOMSBURY ACADEMIC and the Diana logo are trademarks of
Bloomsbury Publishing Plc

First published in Great Britain 2021
Copyright © Nick Bearman, 2021

Nick Bearman has asserted his right under the Copyright, Designs and Patents Act,
1988, to be identified as Author of this work.

For legal purposes the Acknowledgements on p. x constitute an
extension of this copyright page.

Series design by Paul Burgess
Cover image © Eliks/Shutterstock

Bloomsbury Publishing Plc does not have any control over, or responsibility for, any third-
party websites referred to or in this book. All internet addresses given in this book were
correct at the time of going to press. The author and publisher regret any inconvenience
caused if addresses have changed or sites have ceased to exist, but can accept no
responsibility for any such changes.

A catalogue record for this book is available from the British Library.

Library of Congress Cataloging-in-Publication Data
Names: Bearman, Nick, author.
Title: GIS: research methods / Nick Bearman.
Description: London; New York: Bloomsbury Academic, 2020. |
Series: 'What is?' research methods series | Includes bibliographical references and index.
Identifiers: LCCN 2020032080 (print) | LCCN 2020032081 (ebook) |
ISBN 9781350129566 (hardback) | ISBN 9781350129559 (paperback) |
ISBN 9781350129573 (ebook) | ISBN 9781350129580 (epub)
Subjects: LCSH: Geographic information systems. | Spatial analysis (Statistics) |
Social sciences–Geographic information systems. | Social sciences–Research–Methodology.
Classification: LCC G70.212 .B43 2020 (print) | LCC G70.212 (ebook) | DDC 910.285–dc23
LC record available at https://lccn.loc.gov/2020032080
LC ebook record available at https://lccn.loc.gov/2020032081

ISBN: HB: 978-1-3501-2956-6
PB: 978-1-3501-2955-9
ePDF: 978-1-3501-2957-3
eBook: 978-1-3501-2958-0

Series: Bloomsbury Research Methods

Typeset by Deanta Global Publishing Services, Chennai, India

To find out more about our authors and books visit www.bloomsbury.com
and sign up for our newsletters.

Contents

Illustrations

Tables

Series editor's foreword

The idea behind this book series is a simple one: to provide concise and accessible introductions to frequently used research methods and of current issues in research methodology. Books in the series have been written by experts in their fields with a brief to write about their subject for a broad audience.

The series has been developed through a partnership between Bloomsbury and the UK's renowned National Centre for Research Methods (NCRM). The original '*What Is?*' *Research Methods Series* sprang from the eponymous strand at NCRM's Research Methods Festivals.

This relaunched series reflects changes in the research landscape, embracing research methods innovation and interdisciplinarity. Methodological innovation is the order of the day, while still maintaining an emphasis on accessibility to a wide audience. The format allows researchers who are new to a field to gain an insight into its key features, while also providing a useful update on recent developments for people who have had some prior acquaintance with it. All readers should find it helpful to be taken through the discussion of key terms, the history of how the method or methodological issue has developed, and the assessment of the strengths and possible weaknesses of the approach through the analysis of illustrative examples.

This book is devoted to Geographical Information Systems (GIS). In it, Nick Bearman introduces a methodological innovation that in the relatively short time of its existence has been remarkably far-reaching, in several senses. In a literal (spatial) sense, GIS makes it possible for its users to reach into all parts of the globe and to locate and track an enormous range of phenomena, both natural and social. As a consequence, GIS has made the world more knowable than could have been imagined even a generation ago. Nor is this new capacity for knowledge in fine detail restricted to academic enquiry, as is the case with some methodological innovations. GIS is far-reaching in its application by scientists (including social scientists) and lay people alike, a development made possible by its integration into technologies now in widespread everyday use. A further consequence follows from this, as GIS has become a methodological tool that has in turn started to shape people's behaviour. GIS is helping to change our relationship to where we are, that is, to location and to distance, and to social coordination. Like many powerful ideas, the thinking underpinning GIS is relatively simple, although as Nick Bearman shows there is extensive scope for complex knowledge to be derived from its application, and all expectations are that this trend will continue, and quite possibly accelerate. We can also be confident that some degree of understanding of GIS will be required for wide sections of the population to comprehend, and to participate in, large swathes of everyday social and economic activities. By implication, knowledge of GIS will become a key element in the toolkits of researchers in a broad range of academic disciplines.

The books in this series cannot provide information about their subject matter down to a fine level of detail, but they will equip readers with a powerful sense of reasons why it deserves to be taken seriously and, it is hoped, with the enthusiasm to put that knowledge into practice.

Acknowledgements

My thanks to everyone who helped me with this book, including those who first introduced me to GIS many years ago, as well as those who gave me my first opportunities to get into teaching and training. Thanks to both the anonymous reviewers and the series editor who have helped turn this good book into a great book. Thanks also to everyone who I have spoken to about book publishing (both academic and non-academic) and my GIS colleagues across the world. I would particularly like to thank Louise, my wife, who helped me take the big leap, and who has always been there for me.

Introduction

This chapter will introduce the concept of geographical information systems (GIS) and spatial data in general, and set the scene for the book. It will provide pointers for readers about what they can get from the book, and how GIS software can be used in general.

Spatial data underpins our world; after all, everything happens somewhere. Sometimes the use of spatial data is very clear, for example if we are trying to find directions, we need to use spatial data. At other times the use of spatial data is not so obvious, for example when a new supermarket opens near you, the company running it consulted plans and spatial data for land to build the store on, but they also used spatial data to think about who their typical customers were, where they currently shop and where they should place their store to try and get as many customers as possible; spatial data underpins all of this.

This book will show you how we can use spatial data in social science and some of the benefits and insights it can create. While spatial data has been around for a long time, during the last decade it has become much more accessible. This means you don't have to have a master's degree in GIS to be able to get some benefit from spatial data in your research area. With a short course, some reading, or from reading this book, you can start to get the data you have on a map, and realize the potential of GIS.

In Chapter 1 (Using GIS in social science), I will talk about how GIS can be used in social science. I am using the term 'social science' fairly broadly, so this is relevant to everyone. Chapter 2 (The history of GIS) will talk about the history of GIS; we'll cover some interesting background, and it is always useful to know the journey of how we arrived at where we are now. Chapters 3 (Creating maps), 4 (Cartography) and 5 (How is spatial data structured?) cover the nuts and bolts of how GIS works and how we start to go about making maps. These are the key bits of the book. I try to keep the technical theory to a minimum, but there are several key things you need to know, to avoid getting yourself tied up in knots later on. Chapter 6

(Spatial data analysis) discusses how we can progress from plotting data on a map, and to start performing some statistical analysis on the data. It also covers key spatial tools like overlays, a key aspect of spatial analysis. Chapter 7 (GIS software) gives some information on popular GIS software and the different pros and cons of each, and Chapter 8 (Next steps) provides some very brief instructions on using that software, and where to go for more information on each software package.

GIS and map making is as much an art as a science, so do allow your creative side to come out. The vast majority of mapping has no one 'correct' way of doing it – there are different approaches, and one of the key aspects to appreciate is that sometimes you don't know what the right way of doing something is until you try it. The creative element is key to successful map making and cartography, in a very similar way to it being key in data visualization, and there is often crossover between the two fields.

Happy Mapping!

1 Using GIS in social science

Chapter objectives

This chapter will discuss how GIS is used in social science and highlight some case studies from different areas of social science. It will also highlight the limitations of GIS, explain what it cannot do and, in brief, discuss some of the main academic criticisms of GIS.

After reading this chapter you will:

- know what GIS is,
- be aware of how GIS can be used across the social sciences,
- be aware of some of the criticisms of GIS and how these have been addressed and
- know about some of the developments within GIS as a result of Google Earth and OpenStreetMap.

What is GIS?

To start thinking about how we use GIS in social sciences, we first need to consider what GIS is. Geographical information systems or GIS is the use of computers and computerized systems to manage, display and analyse geospatial data. Sometimes systems we use are clearly GIS, for example a satellite-navigation (sat-nav) system is a type of GIS – we enter where we are and where we want to go, and the system calculates the route for us. However, sometimes this is not so obvious, for example when we get vouchers at the supermarket or when a website decides what adverts to show us. The companies use a range of data to work out what vouchers or adverts we might be interested in. This is partly based on our shopping or browser history but also partly based on where we live, which is used to estimate our interests and what we can afford. GIS underpins a whole variety of systems we interact within in our everyday lives – from real-time bus or train information, to traffic light timings, to routing emergency service vehicles.

From a research point of view, GIS is a very valuable way of turning raw data into useful information, and then using this information to answer research questions. The type of research questions that can be answered is almost limitless, and I would say that nearly every area of research can benefit from GIS in some way. Sometimes the relevance of location is fairly clear, for example where people live or where certain animals forage. However, sometimes we need to do some lateral thinking and our location might be the route people take to get from home to work, or it might be the route they take to go to the supermarket. As a rule static locations tend to be easy to work with, but routes are much more complex. For example, taking a trip from London to New York by plane is very different to taking a trip from London to New York on a cruise ship. Sometimes the relevance of space won't be clear at all – for example, in certain branches of mathematics which consider how things are linked together. But there are links with GIS, for example with networks and how different elements are linked together – what mathematics calls graph theory and GIS analysts would call network analysis.

As well as GIS standing for geographical information systems, it can also stand for geographical information science. GISystems are the tools, programs and methods we use to work with geospatial data, and are the main focus of this book. GIScience is the research and creation of new tools and methods, and forms most of the academic area of GIS. We touch on a bit of this in Chapter 6 where we look at spatial data analysis. Sometimes the terms (systems or science) are used interchangeably and the use has changed over time. In 1997, the long-running journal *International Journal of Geographical Information Systems* changed its name to *International Journal of Geographical Information Science* to better reflect the changes in the academic discipline (Yuan, 2017).

GIS has evolved over time, with the barrier to entry (in terms of computer power and technical skill) becoming progressively lower. The launch of Google Earth and Google Maps revolutionized GIS, including explaining what we do to our parents and grandparents ('it's like Google Earth, but you can edit and customize the data, and do analysis'). It also pushed software providers to make their programs much easier to use, which benefits everyone. The history is explored further in Chapter 2.

What is social science?

Now we know what GIS is, how do we apply this in social science? I am being fairly broad in my definition of social science, including anthropology, communication studies, economics, education, history, law, linguistics, political science, psychology, sociology as well as many other areas. Of course, geography is also a key part of social science, but many geographers know GIS already, so if you know GIS already this book is not for you. However, if you are a geographer and want to learn more about GIS, please read on!

Geospatial data is vital in all of these areas and GIS can be applied across them all. For example, economists might look at how people's spending power varies, either at a global scale ('Big Mac Index,' 2019; such as the Big Mac index, 'The Big Mac index', 2019) or within a town or city. In linguistics we might look at how language varies across the world or how it has moved across space and time (Luebbering, 2013). In literature, we might create some very nice maps of fictional worlds, such as the Lord of the Rings or Westeros (Game of Thrones). In public health, we would use GIS to analyse how disease spreads, or how greenspace and bluespace (water) might impact people's health (Foley et al., 2019; Wheeler et al., 2010; White et al., 2016).

John Snow's cholera map

A famous example is from the area of epidemiology or public health, and this is John Snow's cholera map in London (see Figure 1). You may well have seen this already; it is often shown as an example of the very first spatial analysis.

In 1854, John Snow[1] was one of the first people to collect data and plot it onto a map. This allowed him to look at the spatial patterns in the data and make a hypothesis about what was causing these patterns. He plotted people's deaths from cholera on the map, and deduced that deaths appeared to cluster around certain water supplies, with some water supplies having much higher death rates associated with them than others. At the time, the thinking was that cholera was spread by polluted air, rather than through polluted water, as we know now. His plotting of the

---

[1] Note this is John Snow of London, not Jon Snow of Westeros!

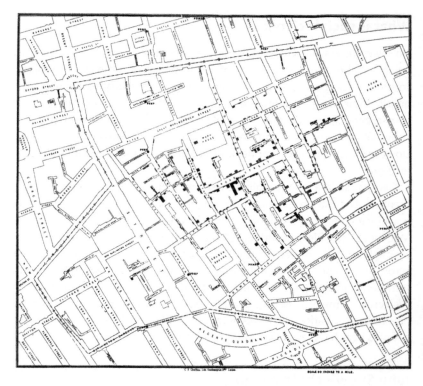

Figure 1 Cholera map around Broad Street, by John Snow.
This is the first spatial analysis where John Snow plotted cases of deaths from cholera around Broad Street, London, UK, in 1854. This map allowed him to link the deaths to a specific water pump and began to confirm the link between cholera cases and contaminated water (*originally from https://en.wikipedia.org/wiki/1854_Broad_Street_cholera_outbreak#/media/File:Snow-cholera-map-1.jpg*).

data onto a map helped deduce the link between the spread of cholera and contaminated water supplies, although the link was not formally recognized until some years afterwards.

Use of GIS in social science: What can and cannot be done

There is a wealth of spatial data available, and a huge amount of insight can be gained across the social sciences. Developments in satellites and machine learning have opened a whole range of satellite imagery possibilities, for example tracking herds of animals across very large areas (Isla Duporge et al., 2019; Naude and Joubert, 2019; Wang et al., 2019). However, with this increased range of data comes an increased range of limitations, for example with satellite data, we have data only when the satellite passes overhead for a specific location. It is also impacted by the angle of the satellite to the earth, and shadows from the angle of the sun, and particularly in temperate climates (e.g. the UK), cloud cover can have a very large impact on how much usable imagery we can get. For example, in the winter in the UK it is not unusual for a third to a half of images to be cloud covered and therefore not usable.

There is also a significant amount of processing to move from raw data to valuable information, which should not be underestimated. A satellite image might show us where a herd of elephants is – but it is us doing the interpretation, and if we have 100 images over 3 years, then we might want the computer to do the interpretation for us. What seems like a simple task for us (finding elephants) is not a simple task for a computer, which needs to be trained (or programmed) to do this. In some cases, novel techniques such as machine learning are very useful in this context and can do a lot of the work for us, but these do have limitations as well.

Data is a key element of any GIS project, and we can have problems of having too much data, insufficient data and the wrong data all in one GIS project. I guarantee you will spend a significant chunk of time in your GIS project trying to find data, trying to find the right data, and converting it into a different format to be able to use it.

One very common type of spatial data to have is people's addresses, or often just their postcodes (e.g. AB1 2EF). Postcodes are a great piece of information because they can locate a house to within a group of ten to twelve dwellings across the whole of the UK in only six or seven characters. They are a great dataset to have, but they do have some limitations which anyone using them needs to be aware of. You probably already know the most common one already, that is, when you type a postcode into a sat-nav, if you are going to a rural location it may well not take you to the house you want to go to. This is because each postcode (what are properly called postcode units, e.g. AB1 2EF) contains ten to twelve dwellings. In an urban setting, this is fine because you probably also know the house number, and can go up or down the road as appropriate, maybe having to cover 100 m or so. However in a rural setting, a postcode still covers ten to twelve dwellings, but the houses are much more widely spaced, and can be over several square kilometres. Compounding this, many houses in rural locations use names rather than numbers, which can make finding them quite tricky to say the least. Therefore, postcodes can give us a very wide range of useful information, but we need to remember their limited precision when working with data in rural locations.

Criticisms of GIS and responses

One major criticism of GIS as an academic discipline was that it was too positivist, relying too exclusively on a computer-based system to capture, analyse and interpret data, and not taking into account additional factors and information that are not included in the GIS. This was specifically an issue in the earlier days of GIS, when it was seen as being technology heavy, and technical specialists would be brought in to solve all your spatial problems with technology. This was criticized as being, at best, inappropriate in many settings and, at worst, harmful, because often the practical upshot was that (particularly in the global south) a big, expensive GIS setup and GIS trained staff would be brought in for a specific project. They would do their work, then either the contract would expire or the money would run out. The staff would leave, and the technology would become outdated with no funding to maintain it. This would then leave whoever was supposed to be benefiting from the technology in much the same situation as they were before the GIS arrived, but with a big database that they couldn't keep up to date or, in the worst cases, even use it at all!

Public participation GIS

As the technological barriers for GIS lowered, more people became involved with a greater range of experiences. An area of GIS called public participation GIS (PPGIS) evolved, developed by geographers (Dunn, 2007). This coincided with a much bigger movement from top-down colonial style involvement in the developing world to bottom-up non-governmental organization involvement, and many of the same strategies and principles were adopted in GIS.

This first gained traction in the rich world particularly in terms of planning applications. Local councils are required to gain engagement from the local community when making planning decisions, for example routing a new road or railway line. Previously this was done through a public planning meeting, where the planners said this is what we have decided, because of x, y and z and this is what we are going to do; hardly a democratic public engagement! Over time, and with pressure from the local communities and academics, this has changed to be a much more focused process actually involving the local population. Typically now residents are given a number of choices (e.g. route A, B or C) and asked to express a preference. The current method is still quite a long way off true engagement (see Figure 2) but it is heading in the right direction.

This positivist attitude among some users of GIS continued for much longer in the developing world. This was partly tied up with Western colonial attitudes, with experts being brought in to use GIS to create a whole range of maps, without really taking into account the local populations. Additionally often these maps were held by government agencies and used to represent or extend their power over the local indigenous populations.

Citizen science

Again, there was a push against this, primarily from the International Development community with the development of a participatory rural appraisal (PRA) – an approach that engages with the local population and works with them to develop maps and spatial data that work with how

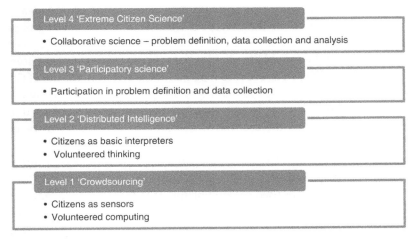

Figure 2 Different levels of engagement are possible through public participation GIS and citizen science (sourced from Haklay, 2013, figure 7.2).

they make use of the natural resources and how they conceptualize space (Allen et al., 2015).

Participatory approaches in both the developed and the developing worlds have been pushed forward by the area of citizen science, using a range of technology (primarily mobile phones with cameras and GPS) to give local citizens the tools to collect data themselves and be involved in a range of scientific research. This has now developed into citizen science, promoting the fact that members of the general public can contribute to scientific research. This has been spearheaded by the extreme citizen science research group at UCL (University College London, UK), who focus on working with marginalized communities in participatory science activities, supporting them to share their indigenous knowledge (Stevens et al., 2014).

This has also been promoted through the development of new data sets, for example WorldPop which is a global gridded population product, designed to enable more people (particularly in developing countries) to make use of current population data and population projections (see www .worldpop.org for more details).

The data divide

The development of both participatory GIS and citizen science has led to and fed off the issue of the so-called data divide. In the general area of social science, this covers the concept of whether or not particular groups have access to certain services and is often linked very closely to class (particularly in the United Kingdom) or race (in the United States). Often, rather than being used as a tool to minimize these divisions, the use of GIS can reinforce and increase these issues by deepening these social divisions. While GIS could be considered a tool, like any tool it has to be used in appropriate ways and the user has to consider the ethics of what she or he is doing (see next section on ethics and privacy). Some of these can also be addressed using GIS, using the techniques and approaches of citizen science, discussed earlier.

A common element used to describe the data divide is that of internet access. With more and more public and private services moving to online provision, and sometimes only available online, having access to the internet is crucial for many aspects of everyday life (Riddlesden and Singleton, 2014;

Singleton et al., 2016). There are certain groups of people who do not have access to online services who then often have to pay a 'not online' premium for their products and services. GIS can be (and has been) used to very easily identify these groups; but the question then is how can the issues raised be addressed? This is a fairly reasonable criticism of GIS, and of science more generally – how can we use our research to make a credible impact that changes some of these issues we have identified? Many of the answers around this require policy makers to actually implement the changes and these are often not straightforward areas to work in.

Ethics and privacy

Ethics is a long-standing issue in GIS (Crampton, 1995; Scull et al., 2016), and there is much to be drawn more widely from geography (Healey and Ribchester, 2019), international development (Hammett et al., 2014), transport (Lucas et al., 2015) and many others. How GIS is used raises a number of questions, both directly, in terms of the people using the GIS as we have discussed already, but also indirectly, in terms of data collection. The surveillance society (Gilliom and Monahan, 2012; Laufs et al., 2020) is something that has been widely discussed, both in academic articles and in the wider press. The computation of data has allowed vast databases of people's information to be collated and analysed, sometimes for very valuable and useful purposes, like public health and medical research. However, sometimes this same technology allows data to be collected and used for less noble causes, like the allegations of electoral interference in the United States, United Kingdom and elsewhere (Johnson, 2019). GIS forms a part of this due to the location data that can be collected by your mobile phone, and then shared with other companies, which can then use the data to analyse where you have been and potentially deduce other information about you.

One of the major issues with the use of these large datasets is the lack of transparency in how they are used. This leads to a lack of understanding about how these work, and then allegations of computers, mobile phones or smart speakers listening to people when advertising starts appearing to people who swear they have only spoken about something, and not (yet) searched for it. The truth of such claims is not confirmed by the evidence, but there is a case for greater transparency regarding how smart speakers process our data (Phelan, 2019; Ruane et al., 2019; Shulevitz, 2018). There was also the case when Target (a big American supermarket) started mailing out pregnancy-related adverts to a family who had a teenage daughter. Her father vocally complained to Target and received a lengthy apology from them. However, it turned out that his daughter was, indeed, pregnant (Hill, 2012). While on the one hand this shows how much 'the system' can know about us, on the other hand, it also shows that we need to implement algorithms with some human restrictions, particularly when dealing with sensitive issues.

The General Data Protection Regulation (GDPR) was implemented in 2018 by the European Union. One of the key aspects of the GDPR is that the user (data subject) has control over what their data is used for, and needs to provide informed consent for their data to be used in this way. GDPR also provides for users to be able to correct data about them if it is wrong. GDPR is still relatively recent and has yet to be fully tested in the courts, although there have been some cases where Google has been fined relatively large amounts (Hern, 2019).

When working with data (including geographic information), researchers have a responsibility for the security of the data they are using. This is both a legal responsibility (through the GDPR) and an ethical responsibility; all ethical reviews will include a section on data security. Researchers are required to follow the appropriate guidance to ensure that data they are working with does not fall into the wrong hands. The specifics of this will, of course, vary depending on what information the data set contains, and most universities and public institutions have guidelines for researchers to follow.

Software developments

The launch of Google Earth in 2005 began the revolution of access to geospatial data. This combined with GIS software being more easily used, and increasing computer power, led to the adoption of GIS across many different academic sectors. While GIS was once a province of environmental science, it now can be used across all of the social sciences. We will discuss this further in Chapter 7.

To use GIS effectively, you need to have access to data for the area you are interested in. Some countries have been relatively open with their spatial data historically (e.g. the United States, but this does vary between states and organizations) whereas others have not. In Great Britain,[2] the national mapping agency is Ordnance Survey, which is run as an arms-length government body. Historically, they received no funding from central government, so are required to fund all of their activities, and previously did this by charging for spatial data, both to commercial clients and government clients. This generated a significant source of revenue but also limited the access to the data to those who could pay (Ordnance Survey, 2019a).

As a result of this, OpenStreetMap was launched which was intended as a global Wikipedia for spatial data; where anyone could add data, and data could be downloaded and used for free, for any purpose (including commercial) (OpenStreetMap, 2019; Wikipedia, 2019). Data was collected by volunteers across the world (part of what we would call now citizen science) and certainly in most developed countries, the accuracy, currency and detail of OpenStreetMap are greater than those of the national mapping agency (Haklay, 2010; Minghini and Frassinelli, 2019).

In Great Britain the most detailed mapping product created by Ordnance Survey is MasterMap. This goes down to a scale of 1:1,000 and is seen as the authoritative data set for Great Britain. This data has been available for academic use to universities though EDINA[3] since 2000 (Ligue des Bibliothèques Européènnes de Recherche, 2003). Until 2010 any public sector users (e.g. local authorities) had to pay to access this data, but in 2010 the Public Sector Mapping Agreement was created, where central government agreed to pay Ordnance Survey a lump sum for all government bodies (local and national) to access MasterMap data (Ministry of Housing, Communities & Local Government, 2010). Until now (2019) a payment was required to use MasterMap data for any commercial use; whether this is a small to medium enterprise (SME) of one to two people or a big publicly traded organization of several thousand employees, the data still has to be paid for.

[2] Great Britain covers England, Scotland and Wales. The United Kingdom is Great Britain (England, Scotland and Wales) and Northern Ireland. For more details, see https://www.historic-uk.com/HistoryUK/HistoryofBritain/The-UK-Great-Britain-Whats-the-Difference/. Ordnance Survey only covers Great Britain. Northern Ireland is covered by Ordnance Survey of Northern Ireland.

[3] https://edina.ac.uk/

The Geospatial Commission was launched in 2018 to open up access to geospatial data across the UK, and one of its key aims was to make MasterMap more accessible (Ordnance Survey, 2019b). They have taken the approach to provide MasterMap data through an API up to a certain threshold – the idea being that this will benefit small businesses and allow them to access the data freely and easily, but still require large companies or those using large amounts of data to pay. At the time of writing (2020) there has been much discussion about what might be launched (Ordnance Survey, 2020), but nothing yet has actually been launched, so we will see what happens.

Summary

This chapter has discussed how GIS is used in social sciences and has shown you some case studies. We have also discussed some of the limitations of GIS, as it is not universally useful and not every problem can be solved with GIS, unfortunately. We also touched on how computer and software development have been key to the adoption of GIS, including the launch of Google Earth. Subsequent chapters will discuss this in more detail. Overall GIS is an incredibly flexible tool with a very wide variety of applications. It can probably be applied in some way to the area you are working on, whether that be cities, planning, politics, history, archaeology or nearly any social science.

2 The history of GIS

Chapter objectives

This chapter will discuss the history of GIS, both from the point of the view of the term 'GIS' (1968) and from the point of the concept of analysing spatial data (John Snow, 1854, among others). Map making forms a part of this history, along with communications and logistics. Separate sections will discuss natural resource management (1963), global positioning systems (GPS) (1997), Google Earth (2005) and big data (early 2010s) in turn, as these signified important changes in how GIS was developed and used.

After reading this chapter you will:

- understand that GIS existed long before the term 'GIS' was invented,
- know about the origins of GIS in natural resource management,
- understand how the provision of GPS/GNSS and Google Earth revolutionized perception and wider use of GIS, and
- realize the impacts of big data in GIS and how this is fundamentally changing how we work with spatial data.

GIS 'pre-history'

Space and location were important for a long time before the term 'GIS' was coined. Maps recording space and location have been around for a long time, at least 8,000 years or so, longer than the written word (Darkes and Spence, 2017). It's hard to say exactly when, because the line distinguishing the 'first map' from an early piece of artwork showing location is quite fine. Many early maps were concerned with depicting the earth, whether as a whole or as large areas of it, rather than focusing on smaller locations such as a town or city.

Using a map as an analytical tool was first done by John Snow, in 1854. Snow plotted a map of an area of London, charting the deaths as a result of cholera and the location of local water pumps. We have already looked at John Snow (see Chapter 1) and his work is often cited as one of the first examples of GIS, in that it was the first to plot data on a map, and use the spatial pattern shown to derive a hypothesis about (in this case) the causes of cholera.

GIS early days – natural resource management

The term 'GIS' and much of its underlying principles were developed by Roger Tomlinson and his colleagues (Tomlinson, 1966). They used their GIS initially in 1963 to build a natural resource digital inventory for Canada. They wanted to create a database of natural resources across the vast areas of Canada. A key element of a GIS is the fact that it is not just a series of maps showing locations but also a database of information linked to this, which allows us to perform spatial queries. It is this database, a key development by Tomlinson, that was vital for their work in Canada, and it is the presence of this database that really defines the data they had and work they were doing as a GIS. While John Snow's cholera map was a really successful piece of spatial analysis, it was not a GIS as such, because there was no database linked to the underlying data on the map. Roger Tomlinson's GIS (originally called Canada Geographic Information System) was used extensively by the Canadian government for continent-wide land management. One of the key elements was that it had a national coordinate system, enabling location to be encoded in a standard way and therefore enabling analysis of the data it held.

The development of commercial GIS began in earnest in the 1970s, with a plethora of names, some of which are still in use today – GRASS GIS (geographic resources analysis support system GIS), Esri[1] and ERDAS. From the 1970s to the 1990s GIS was a niche tool, usually only available to those who add access to powerful mainframe or (later on) desktop computers. As a linked set of maps and database, a GIS was a challenge to run on the computers available at the time and usually required dedicated, higher specification machines to work. Towards the late 1990s, the increased computing power available allowed GIS to be used on a much wider range of machines. This, alongside the development and availability of GPS, more widely available spatial data and the availability of mobile phones with GPS revolutionized the industry, as we shall see.

[1] Originally ESRI (Environmental Systems Research Institute) but now renamed to Esri.

GPS and GNSS

GPS (or Global Positioning Systems) allows us to know what our location is anywhere across the globe, using a small, battery powered, handheld device. This technology is fundamental to the quick and easy acquisition of spatial data, which was a major contribution to making spatial data more widely available. Before GPS, collecting any spatial data was time consuming, necessitating the use of surveying techniques to find and record geographic coordinates, and prone to error, from people transcribing numbers. GPS allows us to quickly and easily collect a whole range of spatial data, usually to an accuracy of about 3 m. By no means is GPS error free compared to surveying, and in many cases, surveying is still required, but for accuracy up to 3 m, GPS is much quicker.

History

Technically, GPS is the name of one system that provides location information. It is one of several global navigation satellite systems (GNSSs), although it was the first by quite a long way, which is why the term 'GPS' is very well known. The system was originally designed and set up by the US military in 1978, with global coverage from 1993. Initially the 'public' signal that was free to use would give you a location accurate to only 100 m or so, and hence was termed 'Selective Availability' (SA) by the US government. The more accurate signal was encrypted, and only the US military (and their allies) used it to get very accurate locations. While US president Bill Clinton (1993–2001) is famous for many reasons, one less well-known piece of legislation he passed was to decrypt the highly accurate GPS signal (National Coordination Office for Space-Based Positioning, Navigation, and Timing, 2007). This was previously only available to the US military, but after his changes, it was available for everyone. Accuracy is relative here – going from an accuracy of a few hundred metres to tens of metres makes the GPS signal so much more useful. To borrow the US example: 'As illustration, consider a football stadium. With selective availability activated, you really only know if you are on the field or in the stands at that football stadium; with SA switched off, you know which yard marker you are standing on' (Milbert, 2000). This increased accuracy, coupled with the increase in computer power and more widely available spatial data, was key to revolutionizing the spatial data industry across the world. One other consequence of this was that the time signal within the GPS (which is vital to calculating the location) has also been used to very accurately synchronize clocks across many different regions, which is one of the reasons that the world is so reliant on GPS today (Van Sickle, 2015).

Beyond GPS

While the US GPS is the most well-known GNSS, there are a number of other systems that have been developed over the years and are in varying states of operation. The newest (and probably the most well known, certainly within Europe) is the European Union's Galileo system. This has been in development since 2005, and provides a much more accurate positioning system (1 m, compared with 3 m for GPS) than GPS, with a range of different uses for emergency and military users, as well as civilian use (De Ingenieur, 2018). There are also a range of public sector and commercial signals which can be much more accurate, up to 20 cm.

The only other GNSS in global working order is GLONASS (Globalnaya navigatsionnaya sputnikovaya sistema, or GLObal NAvigation Satellite System), developed and run by the Russian Federation. There are a number of other systems with regional coverage, including BeiDou (China), Quasi-Zenith (Japan) and Indian regional navigation satellite system (IRNSS). These are in varying levels of development. These are operational at a regional level, covering their country of origin and surrounding areas (Van Sickle, 2015).

Each GNSS system can be used independently, and they can also be used together. During the 2010s and the 2020s, mobile phones have been and are being developed with the capability to receive multiple signals from different GNSS systems. This will provide higher levels of accuracy and reliability, reducing the reliance on the US-based GPS.

How it works

GPS (or GNSS) works by receiving a signal from three or more satellites in orbit. This signal consists of a very accurate time signal from an atomic clock on-board each of the satellites. By calculating the difference between these three (or more) signals, the receiver can work out it's location(s) is possible, given the difference between the signals (by the different time in the different signals, given that the signal moves at the speed of light, which is a constant). The principles of trigonometry GPS uses are exactly the same as how we may have used *sin, cos* or *tan* to work out the sizes of triangles in school, but a bit more advanced because we are dealing with very accurate times (and therefore distances). This is one of the reasons why the accuracy of the atomic clocks is so important and why 'leap seconds' become very important. If the unit can get signals from more than three satellites (GPS or other systems), then it can start to calculate error in the signal and derive a much more accurate location.

Accuracy

Using a standard, handheld unit or GPS on your mobile phone, location from GPS is accurate to about 3 m–5 m. Systems such as Galileo are going to provide more accuracy (up to 20 cm) but have only recently been completed, and the sensors required to use them are not widely available in mobile phones. If you need more accurate information than this, then generally you need to spend more money. A real-time kinematic (RTK) GPS uses a base station and a survey pole. The base station is located in one position for a number of hours and collects GPS data over this period. It can then work out its location accurately down to 1–2 cm or sometimes even mm, depending on how good the GPS signals are. The surveyor carries around a handheld unit (sometimes a pole with a disc at the top) which then talks to the base unit, and records very accurate locations by combining data from the base unit with the GPS signals it receives.

Depending on the environment you are collecting data in, signals can be impacted by multi-path issues – for example, this happens when you are in a big city and in an 'urban canyon' between a number of skyscrapers. Either you will just get very limited signals, or you might pick up signals reflected off tower blocks, which can interfere with getting an accurate location, because the timing of the signal isn't accurate, but the GPS unit has no way of knowing that the signal has bounced off a tower block (Gong et al., 2012).

Accuracy is not the be all and end all, and there are other ways of working out your location. For example, your Android phone uses GPS, but Google also have a massive database of Wi-Fi points, and uses a similar sort of trigonometry to use those to increase your location's accuracy (Nur et al., 2013). This is particularly useful in indoor environments (e.g. a shopping centre) where you can't receive a GPS signal.

Google Earth

When Google Earth was first launched in 2005, it revolutionized how easy it was to access spatial data. Before this, you could access spatial data only by using specialized software and dedicated systems, usually at big companies, universities or government organizations. After 2005, anyone with an internet connection could download and install Google Earth and browse around the globe to their heart's content. Google soon launched a version of this as Google Maps, with more focus on spatial data and navigation. This is when the platform moved from a novel product to something that many people use every day, such as directions/route finding. Google Maps provided a great, easy-to-use interface to spatial information for anyone with an internet connection. When this was combined with a mobile phone with a GPS chip and mobile data access, it allowed people out and about access to mapping data very easily. Google used the wide availability of Android phones to collect a wide range of real-time traffic information for Google – by having each phone reporting its location and how fast it was moving – which Google could then integrate into their navigation application. The ease of use combined with real-time traffic information more or less killed off standalone sat-navs for general usage. The collection of this data creates a whole range of privacy issues, which we will discuss in the next section.

Google Street View was another big development, where 'street level' images and information were made available to the public. Instead of using aerial, satellite and existing data sets, here Google decided to collect this data using their own Street View cars, providing quite a sight when they did, and also providing the opportunity for people to pose for Street View images. The Google mapping environment is primarily designed for viewing rather than editing data. It is possible to add your own data to Google Earth/Maps, using either Google My Maps or KML files, but it is a bit of a clunky and limiting process. To edit data easily and at scale, this is where a GIS comes in.

For me, the launch of Google Earth was the big stepping stone, and the move from Google Earth to Google Maps was a move from an interesting, novel project to a really useful product. Google as a whole have revolutionized the access to spatial data, and the ease of use of their products has driven a whole range of changes in the GIS community.

GIS and big data

Since 2015, much has been talked about big data, that is, data that has more observations and/or more variables than we are used to, typically millions of observations and/or hundreds of variables. Much of this big data comes from unusual sources, for example loyalty card data, tweets or mobile phone location data (each of which can have tens of millions or hundreds of millions of observations). Much of the information about big data varies depending on what field you are working in and therefore what specific type of data you are using.

When it comes to spatial data, big data is not particularly unusual, depending on how different people define 'big'. The most common types of big data involve hundreds or thousands of rows of data, often transaction based. One of the most unusual sorts of big data, which can be the most difficult to work with, is temporal data, and often this can have quite a fine temporal resolution (e.g. an observation every twenty-five seconds). Over a year, this can add up to a very large number of observations (~2.1 million), and if you have this data for a number of different locations, the numbers get very large very quickly.

Data science is the area of expertise that makes use of big data. Being able to use coding languages (such as R or Python) is key to getting the most out of these data sets. It has only been for a few years that 'coding' has become important in mainstream GIS – prior to this, coding was the preserve of computer scientists. This expansion of coding is only going to continue and will become a vital skill set in any area that wants to make use of data sets. If geographers (and social scientists) don't have the skill sets (of coding and programming) to create new tools to analyse these data, then it will be left to others to create tools for us to use, and we won't have much say in the creation of these tools (Singleton, 2014).

Summary

The use of GIS has changed throughout its history and will continue to do so. For a significant period GIS was limited by the technology available, but now computer processing power is generally not a problem. Now the limits of GIS are mostly to do with data and our conceptual understanding of the issues involved. The technology we use with GIS will continue to change and while we can teach users now how to use R or Python, it is also vital to teach them how to learn new programming languages and techniques as they come along, as new languages and approaches are being developed all of the time.

3 Creating maps

Chapter objectives

In this chapter we will discuss different types of maps and provide some examples of where and when each type should be used. We will discuss context maps and choropleth maps, including different methods of classifying data for choropleth maps and pitfalls to avoid when creating choropleth maps. We will also discuss the case for using rates of data rather than raw count data to create a map with a more useful message.

After reading this chapter you will:

- understand there are many different ways we can show data on a map,
- be aware of the different types of maps we can produce,
- understand the use of colour and classification systems in choropleth maps, and
- be aware of why using rate data is much more useful than using count data.

Map types and variables

There are many different types of maps and many different ways of showing data on a map. Much like the different projection systems, no particular map design is 'wrong'; they just each have their own advantages and disadvantages, and can be more or less appropriate in different situations.

There are also many different ways of showing data on a map. MacEachren (1994) summarized these as follows:

- size
- value
- hue

- saturation
- orientation
- shape
- arrangement
- texture
- focus

Each of these can be used in different ways to show different data. Some of these are more or less appropriate for points, lines or polygons and often they are used in combination, for example motorways on most maps are coloured blue (to match the signs) and also a thicker line is used to represent them (the line used for motorways is thicker than the line used for A roads).

Each one of these is useful in different situations, and some are much better at showing certain types of data than others. One nice example of using direction is the use of a series of arrows to show tidal flow in a map. The colour and size of the arrows is used to show the strength of flow (using two variables to show one set of data is quite a common approach, and reinforces that element of the data). The design allows you to get a good overview of the map as a whole, as well as looking at specific sections in detail (see Figure 3).

There are many other examples of maps on the web, and often the best way of getting design ideas is to look at other people's maps. Often the best maps are a mixture of science and art, and there is a whole chapter (Chapter 4) on cartography in this book – how we go about making maps that look good and are really useful. Over the rest of this chapter we will pick out a couple of common map types and highlight some key information about them and why they are useful.

Context maps

One of the most common types of map is a context map. This map shows where a study area is or the area of your analysis. Essentially it shows the context of your study, hence the name. These are very useful when your audience is not familiar with the area you are showing on the map and they can provide the setting for your map.

Often they are used for maps of small areas that are likely not to be familiar to the audience. For example, when I was working on some data

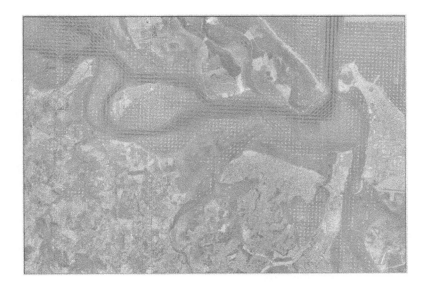

Figure 3 An example of using colour and direction to show tidal flow. Tauranga harbour tidal movements, Bay of Plenty, NZ; the arrows indicate speed (colour) and direction (orientation) (courtesy: Esri). *https://present5.com/terrestrial-topographic-map-of-whistler-british-columbia-canada/*.

in an area of Tanzania, I created a context map that showed both where the area was in Tanzania and where Tanzania was in Africa. Whether this is needed or not depends on your audience and their existing geographical knowledge (see Figure 4).

Choropleth maps

Another very common type of map is a choropleth map, and this is where colours are used to show how values of a variable vary across space (see Figure 5).

These maps are fundamental to many types of spatial analysis, and we can use them to show many different types of data. They are also a great way to show your data in a consistent format if you are comparing data sets across time or different data sets across the same spatial area.

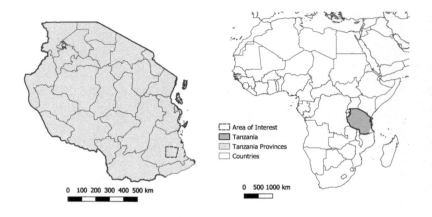

Figure 4 A context map, showing an area of interest within Tanzania, and also the location of Tanzania within Africa. *Data for Tanzania Provinces from GADM database (www.gadm.org), version 3.4, April 2018. Country outlines from Natural Earth (www.naturalearthdata.com).*

We need two key bits of information for a choropleth map: a table of data grouped into certain geographic zones (these can be any type of zones, for example countries, counties, states, wards, etc.) and a set of spatial data showing where the geographic zones are. We then link these two sets of data by using a piece of information that is common to them both, usually the name (e.g. a country's name) or a code (e.g. a LSOA[1] code). This then allows us to link each row of data with a specific geographic zone. We can then colour these geographic zones to create our choropleth map.

There are three of key questions we need to think about when we create a choropleth map: (1) How many different groups of data do we have? (2) What values do these groups cover? (3) Which colours do we use in the map to show those groups?

The number of groups we have can vary, but good practice is usually between five and seven groups. We need to have enough groups that we can gain some distinction between the colours, but not too many that we can't tell the different colours apart. For example, if we had twelve different

---

[1] LSOA, Lower layer Super Output Area, a key geography that UK Census data is provided in. See https://www.ons.gov.uk/methodology/geography/ukgeographies/censusgeography for more details.

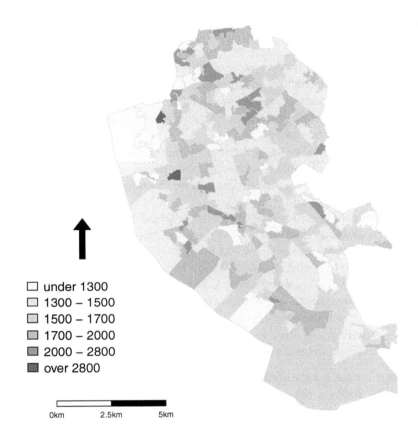

under 1300
1300 – 1500
1500 – 1700
1700 – 2000
2000 – 2800
over 2800

0km   2.5km   5km

Figure 5 A choropleth map showing the total population of Liverpool City, UK, by LSOA. *Contains National Statistics data © Crown copyright and database right (2020). Contains OS data © Crown copyright (2020).*

groups and were using shades of blue, it would probably be quite difficult to distinguish each individual shade of blue. Five groups is usually a good starting point, but this can be varied if there are certain reasons within the data for there to be a specific number of groups. For example, you would use four groups if the data were split into quarters (four categories) or you might have ten groups if the data were split into deciles (ten categories, e.g. Index of Multiple Deprivation [IMD]).

We also need to decide which values these groups cover, for example whether the ranges are 0–10, 11–20, 21–30, 31–40 and so on or something different. The following are a number of different approaches we could use:

- Equal Interval is when we look at the range of the data (difference between maximum and minimum) and then split this between however many groups we want. For example, if data ranges from 0 to 100, and we wanted 5 groups, the ranges would be 0–20, 21–40, 41–60, 61–80 and 81–100.
- Quantile is when we put the same number of data points in each group. For example, if we had 200 data points, and wanted 4 groups, we would put the first 50 data points in group 1, the second 50 in group 2 and so on.
- Standard Deviation is when we use the spread of the data to define the classification intervals. We use the mean of the data as a mid-point, then have categories from −2.5 SD to < −1.5 SD, −1.5 SD to < −0.5 SD, −0.5 SD to < +0.5 SD, +0.5SD to < +1.5 SD and +1.5 SD to +2.5 SD.
- Natural Breaks (Jenks/Fisher) is where we use a function to allocate the groups based on the data. It minimizes the within group difference and maximizes the between group difference. It is based on k-means clustering and uses an iterative process to calculate the optimal classification breaks (Esri, 2005; Jenks, 1967).

When choosing a classification method, the best rule of thumb is to use Natural Breaks – this creates the best balance between ensuring spatial variation on the map and creating sensible classes. If you have a good reason to adjust the breaks, then you can do so. For example, if you were plotting data on a change from the mean, then you could have your mean value as a class, and above the mean in shades of red and below the mean in shades of blue. Or if you were plotting temperature data, it might make sense to have a break in classes at 0°C.

When creating your maps, experiment with the different options of classification to see what impact it has on the map. There is not necessarily a 'right' or 'wrong' answer regarding which classification to use, it is just that some are more appropriate than others. Ultimately you have to make a decision about what is the best method for showing your data. It is important to think about which classification method you use because different methods can make the same data look quite different (see Figure 6).

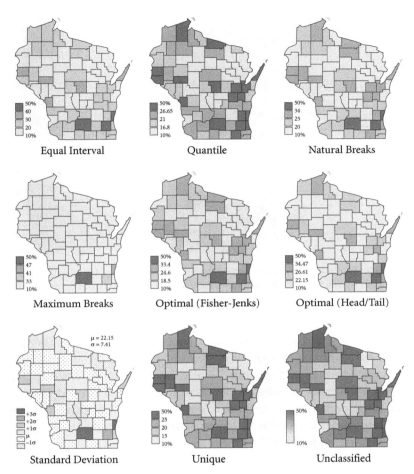

Figure 6 Different types of classification methods used in choropleth maps.
Image based on https://gistbok.ucgis.org/sites/default/files/CV05_Fig11.png.

The final issue to consider when creating choropleth maps is colour. We need to use different colours to show the different groups on the map, but of course the question is which colours should we use?

We want our map to be easy to read and need the colours to be distinguishable, so the map user can see which classification group each geographic zone is in. Cynthia Brewer has done a wide range of work in

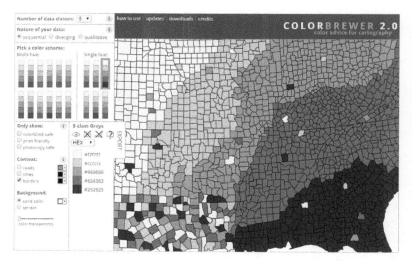

Figure 7 An example of a black-and-white colour scheme from ColorBrewer. *Copyright (c) 2002 Cynthia Brewer, Mark Harrower and The Pennsylvania State University.*

colour theory, and has a very useful website, ColorBrewer.org (Brewer, 2019; Harrower and Brewer, 2003). This site gives us a demonstration of a choropleth map and suggests suitable colours for different mapping options. You can select what shades of colour you would like, and whether you are representing a continuous series or categorical data. You can also select whether you have a univariate range of colours (one range) or bivariate (e.g. above or below a mean value) (see Figure 7).

Using rate data

When creating choropleth maps, we have seen how big the variety of options is. There is one other aspect to think about – the actual data we are showing. So far we haven't considered this at all, but it is very important.

When creating choropleth maps, we usually have the option of using count data or rate data. Count data is the number of objects within each geographic zone (e.g. the number of people aged under sixteen, or the number of people with a certain health condition). If we just plotted these numbers, this would be adequate, but not necessarily the greatest of maps.

This is because if our geographic zones are of varying sizes then this needs to be taken into account. When I say *size* here, I mean both the geographic area and population within the zone.

For example, if we are looking at country level data, 1,000 people suffering from a certain condition is very different in the United States compared to Luxemburg, for example. This is because the populations for the countries are very different: the United States' is 327 million (2018) and Luxemburg's is 519,000 (2017). What we are really more interested is the rate – so number of cases per 10,000 population (0.03 for the United States and 19.3 for Luxemburg – very different!).

So when we are creating choropleth maps, it is very important to use rates rather than counts. If the geographic zones vary drastically in terms of the denominator for our calculation (usually population) then this is very important. If the geographic zones are consistent (or mostly consistent) in terms of the denominator (e.g. LSOA boundaries which each contain about 1,500 people, or output areas [OAs] which each contain about 100 households) then you can get away with using count data (because the data is still comparable) but it is still best practice to use rate data.

Summary

When we are creating any type of map in our GIS, there are numerous data-related issues to consider. The list in this chapter is a good starting point for anyone new to making maps, highlighting what you need to think about. It is not exhaustive, and there are more design-related items in the chapter on cartography (Chapter 4). The more maps you create, the easier this process will be and the more options, designs and styles you will explore. There is no one 'right' design for a particular set of data – just some that are more or less appropriate. You need to critically look at the maps you design and think about why you are making the decisions you choose for the classification methods.

4 Cartography

If you are using GIS to show some data on a map, it is important that the map is legible and easy for both the creator of the map and the end users of the map to understand. Cartography, which has sometimes been described as both a science and an art, is the area that provides the skills and techniques to make this possible. We will cover a range of examples, hints and tips and common pitfalls to avoid.

The single most important piece of advice I can give here is to look at other people's work – this is by far the best way of getting design ideas, and there are so many examples of different maps out there, all of which can provide amazing inspiration. The great ones will make you think about using those techniques with your data; the less good ones will show you things and layouts you want to avoid.

After reading this chapter you will:

- be aware of what makes a good map,
- understand that a map is not always the best way to show spatial data,
- be able to understand what message you want your map to communicate and
- know what key elements are needed on a map.

What makes a good map?

The key element of a good map is that it can be easily read. A map is no good if whoever is looking at it can't get the information they need from it. One of the most common problems with maps is trying to include too much information on it. The map gets cluttered and then it is difficult to see anything easily on it.

It is very tempting to say 'that's amazing, can we just add this bit of information to the map?', to which the answer is probably yes, but whether you should add that bit of extra information or not is another question. There is a limit to how much you can show on a map and trying to pack more information onto it will not end well. Most likely you will overload the user of the map with too much information and they won't be able to see anything at all on the map; 'they will not be able to see the wood for the trees'. Therefore, it is necessary to prioritize what is included on the map – 'less is more', as they say.

Do you even need a map?

Depending on what spatial data you are showing, sometimes you don't even need a map. It depends on how much the spatial element adds to the understanding of the data. Sometimes the spatial element is vital and so we need to show the data on a map. At other times, it might just get in the way. For example, if we are dealing with a small number of spatial units (e.g. government office regions, eleven in the UK) then often the spatial element doesn't add much at all. However, if we want to see how a value varies across the UK and we have data at local authority level (326 in the UK) then the spatial element is probably very important. As a map designer, you have to make this call about how best to present the information. This is a skill that comes with experience and looking at how other people have presented their data and whether this works or not.

When working with temporal data, it is very hard to show spatial data and temporal data on a static map. Often animation is used, which is tricky to implement, but can work very well for some data (Datanovia, 2019; Faber, 2018). When working with temporal data, sometimes it is a good idea to ignore or remove the spatial element completely, and work around a linear output based on time, or a more one-dimensional view of distance. For example, many plots of Gross Domestic Product (static and animated) use country level data, so are inherently spatial, but they are usually not shown on a map.

The message of your data

When putting together a map, the message the map is trying to convey needs to be clear. What are you aiming for people reading the map to be able to get from it?

- Are you trying to show there is a pattern in your data?
- That certain areas have high values and certain areas have low values?

- That people should be able to use your map to find where they are/ where they are going to?
- To get a general understanding of the spatial spread of the data?
- Is the map something to look amazing that hangs on the wall?
- To show how a complex transport system works and how different lines interconnect?

Whatever the aim of your map, it needs to be clear. One of the best tips is to show your map to someone who hasn't seen it before, and ask what they think. It is so easy to get absorbed into the finer points of the map, that you see what you think is there, and miss errors on the map. This is exactly like proofreading an essay – if you've been working on it for a long time, you see what you think is there, rather than what is actually there. Having a 'critical friend' is very important here – someone who will give you critical, constructive feedback. This will help you make your map better, and mostly likely save you time in the long run.

Key elements on a map

The following are a number of elements that are often found on maps:

- Title/caption
- Legend
- Scale
- North arrow
- Copyright and/or acknowledgement

Not all of these are required on every map; like many things, it depends on the map.

A title is usually required, but the shorter the better. There is no need to say 'A map of . . .' as it should be obvious it is a map. The title should cover the data being shown and the geographic area of the map. If you are putting your map in an essay or journal article, then you will have a caption, and therefore you will not need a title.

The legend (or key) should explain what the colours and/or symbols on the map represent. The level of detail required can vary, but the important aspect is for it to be clear. One quick check you can do to improve your map is, are all the symbols on the map in the key, and are all the symbols in the key on the map?

A scale shows what area your map covers and allows the reader to know how big things are. This is often represented using a scale bar or sometimes

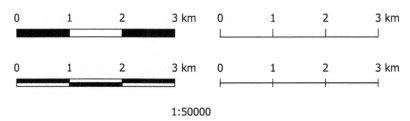

Figure 8 A scale bar, showing how far different distances are on the map. Different styles shown are Single Box, Double Box, Line Ticks Up, Line Ticks Middle and Numeric.

as a ratio, such as 1:50,000. Using this style works only on printed maps, and means that 1 unit on the final printed product is 50,000 units in the real world. For example, 1 cm on a printed map would be 50,000 cm in the real world (i.e. 500 m) (see Figure 8).

On web maps, sometimes scale bars are not shown. Due to the dynamic nature of webmaps, it can be tricky to show scale bars that vary as the user zooms in or out, but because of this dynamic nature, I would say that scale bars are much more important. Otherwise is can be very difficult to know how big a feature showing on the web map actually is in reality. Is this lump in the sand a small hill I can climb over, or a massive sand dune that I will need to drive around?

A north arrow is an optional extra, in some cases not relevant at all, and in some cases very relevant. Looking at a global representation or a map covering the North Pole or the South Pole, a north arrow is irrelevant. When showing smaller areas, conventionally north is assumed to be 'up', but often for a printed map, the map is rotated to fit better on a piece of paper, so in these cases a north arrow is very important. Some map designers have made a feature of this and there are many maps of the world with Australia at the 'top', and a deliberately designed map with the Mediterranean 'upside down'. North does not have to be up – this is merely convention, and convention can be ignored sometimes! (see Figure 9).

All maps are likely to need some copyright or acknowledgement statement on them. When using certain data sets, the data supplier will require you to include a copyright statement on your map, for example, using Ordnance Survey OpenData you need to include 'Contains OS data © Crown copyright [and database right] [year]', or if you are using OpenStreetMap data, you need to include '© OpenStreetMap contributors'.

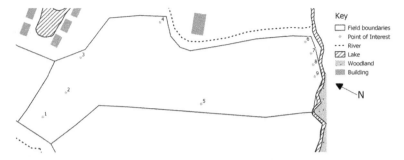

Figure 9 A site map, rotated so that more detail can be shown on the map. Note how the north arrow indicates that the map has been rotated from the traditional 'north is up' design. *Map created by Nick Bearman using OS Open Map Local Data © Crown copyright and/or database right 2020 OS.*

It is also good practice to cite your data sources in this section, exactly the same as you would in an academic paper. You can also add any additional information, such as your name, email, date, institution and any other relevant information. If your map is part of a larger product (essay or poster) you can incorporate some of this information into the main text or elsewhere; however the copyright statements should be clearly associated with each map.

Map hints and tips

The following are my top tips for better maps:

- For choropleth maps, don't use the default equal interval classification scheme; Jenks or Natural Breaks is usually a lot better.
- Depending on your data, potentially adjust the class intervals to round numbers, and remove any decimal places if they are not relevant.

Example	Improved Example
0–42.5	0–49
42.5–72.5	50–74
72.5–99.5	75–99
99.5–137	100–149
137–200.5	150–199
200.5–256	200–250

- Use a colour palette from Color Brewer.
- Be aware of the potential impact of people's colour blindness and avoid red-green colour scales.
- Check the legend; are all the symbols on the map in the legend and all the symbols in the legend on the map?
- Print the map and proofread a physical copy.
- Get a second opinion on the map layout.

One of the best texts on cartography I have come across is Darkes and Spence's (2017) *Cartography: An Introduction*. It gives a great overview of map design and includes hundreds of examples of great maps, and shows how you can make changes to good maps to make them amazing.

5   How is spatial data structured?

Chapter objectives

This chapter will discuss how spatial data is structured and the process by which we take information from the real world and store this information as a model on a computer. There are several implications to be discussed from how spatial data is recorded and stored, and what the implications are for using this data. Specific sections will discuss projections and coordinate systems (the most common cause of problems in GIS projects) and how we go about accessing spatial data.

After reading this chapter you will:

- understand how spatial data is stored in a computer,
- be aware of why projections and coordinate systems are important for spatial data,
- understand what implications specific projections and coordinate systems have for spatial data and
- be aware of different methods of storing spatial data and know which ones to use in different situations.

Storing spatial data

The world is an infinitely complex entity and if we want to map part of the world in some way, we have to limit the amount of information and detail of information that we store. Any map we create is inherently a model of the world – a simplified representation. We have to simplify it because we cannot create a 100 per cent accurate detailed model, because this would be far too big and too detailed to store either in paper or in digital form.

When we decide to create a model of the real world, we have various decisions to make. A part of this is what we include in our model and what we do not include. For example, do we include that field boundary? Do we include whether it is a fence, hedgerow, ditch or just the fact that it is a boundary? Many of the answers to these questions depend on what we are going to use the data for, that is, why are we collecting it? There are some instances where whether the field boundary is a fence or a ditch is important, and there are other instances where it isn't important at all. This is why when we are using spatial data that someone else has collected for us (which is almost all of the time) we have to ask 'Is the data appropriate for what we want to use it for?'

Another decision we have to make is how we are going to model our data. In GIS we have two different approaches of modelling data. We can model the world either as discrete objects or as a continuous field. These are usually mutually exclusive (i.e. data has to be one or the other) and are *usually* linked to either vector data (discrete objects) or raster data (continuous field), but more on this later.

If we model data as a series of discrete objects, then we are saying that each object has a well-defined boundary, and outside of the objects is empty space. As a rule, each object has to occupy a different space, and you can't have two objects sharing space. For example, this works very well for building footprints, field boundaries and roads. If we model data as a continuous field, we are saying we have this variable that has values across the whole world, and has a value at every possible location. For example, this works very well with height data, land cover, population and land ownership.

As you have probably guessed, each approach has advantages and disadvantages. Most of the time you don't get a choice of the format of the data you are using. It is possible to convert between formats, and if you are using multiple data in different formats, then this is often required. Usually discrete objects are implemented in a GIS as vector data, and continuous field data is implemented as raster data. However, you do sometimes get continuous data that is implemented in a vector format (e.g. continuous grids, triangular irregular networks and some land ownership data where there is continuous coverage). Very occasionally you can get discrete objects implemented as raster data (e.g. roads or rivers) but this is exceptional, and usually data has been converted from vector to raster for processing within a larger piece of analysis (see Figure 10).

Most of the time data in a GIS is split into either vector or raster data. Vector data is split into three subtypes: point, line and polygon. Points are

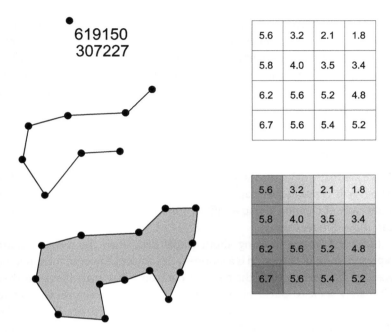

Figure 10 Spatial data types, left: vector data, points, lines and polygons; right: raster data.

a single location, represented by one pair of coordinates. We might use this to represent the location of a person, a data sample point or a town. Lines are made up of a series of points, linked together. We use these to represent linear features, such as roads, rivers or railways lines. Polygons are a series of points linked together which then links back on itself to enclose the space. We would use these to represent areas, such as country boundaries, administrative boundaries and land parcels. Polygon data are a key element of a choropleth map – they are used to represent the geographic zones.

Raster data uses a continuous grid to represent data. Each cell is a set size, its resolution. Usually the cells are square (although they don't have to be) and resolutions can vary from 100 m, 10 m, all the way down to 25 cm or smaller. The value in each cell represents the data, and typical examples of raster data could be height, land cover, rainfall, average temperature or soil type. Satellite (or remotely sensed) data is a specific subset of raster data, where the values in each cell represent the reflectance value in certain wavelengths. Satellite data can be really useful and contain a wide range of data – both from the visible wavelengths (what we can see) and invisible wavelengths (such as thermal or infrared). As well as allowing us to see what the world looks like (to us), this can also help us understand heat loss, vegetation growth, moisture levels and a whole range of other information.

Projections

There are many different ways of showing spatial data, depending on what whoever is creating the map is trying to achieve. In fact, there is no one 'right' way of creating a map – different maps have different purposes and can show different things.

Indeed, if we are thinking about global data, then the most accurate representation of the world is a globe – a 3D object. However, most people want to be able to view their global data on a flat map (because they ultimately want to put it on a flat piece of paper). Therefore we have to change the data from a 3D globe to fit on a flat piece of paper. The term for this is called 'projecting' and there are many different ways of doing this. Have a look at two examples in Figure 11.

The two images in Figure 11 both show the world, but in a very different way. Compare the sizes of Africa and Greenland: in the Mercator projection they look about the same size. However we know that Africa is about 30 million km^2, and Greenland is about 2 million km^2 – very different in size! In the Gall-Peters projection, they look very different, in fact they are much more representative of their size in the real world, and this is intentional. Different projections are used for different reasons, and when we are going from a 3D sphere to a flat map, we cannot maintain all aspect of the data, that is, we can't maintain the shape, area and angles of the countries. Something has to be distorted in order to be able to transform the 3D globe onto a flat map.

The Mercator projection was designed in 1569 by Gerardus Mercator, a Flemish cartographer. It was designed for trans-ocean navigation, and so the angles (or bearings) on the map were kept correct. This allows navigators to take readings of the map to plot the course for their ships. Maintaining the angles meant that the shape and area of the countries had to be distorted, which distorted the size of Africa and Greenland as we saw earlier. The Gall-Peters projection was designed to maintain the land area of each country.

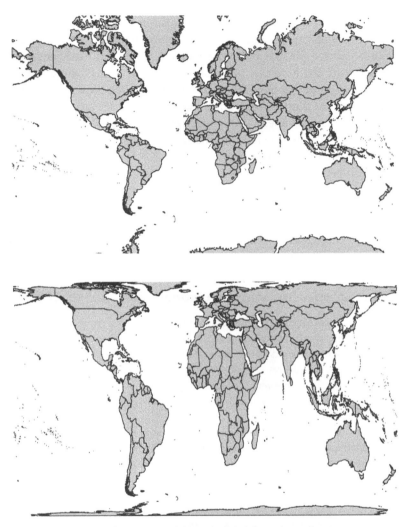

Figure 11 Two very different ways of showing global data, above the Mercator projection, below the Gall-Peters project. *Data from Natural Earth.*

Therefore the shape and angles of each country were distorted, which makes the countries look 'different' to what we are used to.

The most accurate visualization of the world is of course a globe. So if you can use a globe, do. The Mercator projection was very popular for a long time, and was the main design used for global maps in schools for many years, which is why it looks so familiar to us. It even featured on 'The West Wing'![1] It was also very popular in web maps, partly because it is much easier to handle and process than a globe, and partly because a few tweaks to the Mercator projection makes the maths behind it much less complex, and therefore easier to run within a web browser (Battersby et al., 2014). For a long time, Google Maps used it as their base map (and OpenStreetMap still does – go to openstreetmap.org and zoom out as far as you can). Google have recently changed to a globe view – try going to maps.google.com and zoom right out.

Projections are important because they impact how the map looks, particularly for global data. For data covering smaller areas (e.g. a small country) they are almost irrelevant – which projection we use will make little difference to how the map looks. However, they are very closely related to coordinate systems, which are very important for a map of any scale, covering any area.

Cartograms – showing population rather than space

While physical space is the most common representation on maps, it is not the only way of representing data and often not the best. For example, when we are showing data that relates to people, such as election results or deprivation measures, it makes sense to rescale the map to population rather than space. One very popular method of doing this is a cartogram (see Figure 12), which has been popularized by the work of Danny Dorling (Dorling, 1994).

This approach is also often taken with election results, as using a geographical view makes the geographically larger rural constituencies much more prominent than the smaller urban constituencies (Field, 2015). In countries such as the United Kingdom and the United States, where often there is a trend for urban areas to elect one party and rural areas to elect another party, this can massively visually over-represent whichever party is dominant in rural areas. Sometimes a cartogram is used, and sometimes hexagons are used to represent each seat; the ideal being the same, to represent each seat equally. Cartograms can be created easily and I have used the software ScapeToad (http://scapetoad.choros.place/) successfully before[2] (see Figures 13 and 14).

[1] https://www.youtube.com/watch?v=vVX-PrBRtTY.

[2] See also https://go-cart.io/ for creating simple cartograms on the web and https://worldmapper.org/faq/#8 for other software options.

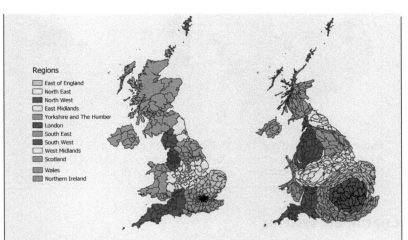

Figure 12 On the left, a standard geographic map of the UK, showing the different regions. On the right, a cartogram version, adjusted to show population. For example, London (bottom right) is much larger to show there are many more people living there, and parts of Scotland (top) are much smaller because of their much lower population. *Population data and boundary source: Office for National Statistics licensed under the Open Government Licence v.3.0, Contains OS data © Crown copyright and database right 2020. Cartogram created using ScapeToad v1.1, http://scapetoad.choros.place/.*

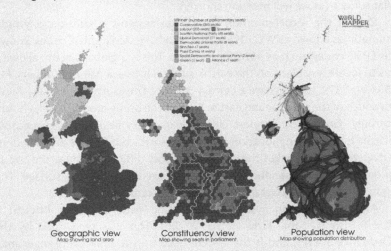

Figure 13 2019 election results of the UK shown in standard geographic view (L), hexagon view (C) and cartogram view (R). The hexagon view is ideal because each constituency covers a variable geographic area and has a variable population, but each constituency is equally important when forming a majority in the House of Commons.

Figure 14 The United States has similar issues with election data as the UK. A cartogram can more accurately represent the relative amount of Democrat (light grey) vs. Republican (dark grey) votes (Newman, 2016).

Coordinate systems

There are many thousands of different coordinate systems. Most likely you will probably end up using only two or three when working with spatial data, and we will cover the key ones here that you are likely to come across. We can split coordinate systems into two groups – geographic coordinate systems, which view the world as a globe (as mentioned previously), and projected coordinate systems, which view a small section of the globe as a flat surface (as we will mention shortly).

One of the most common coordinate systems is latitude/longitude, sometimes known as WGS 1984. They also have snappy little codes, known as EPSG codes, such as 4326 for this one. This is a global system, allowing us to locate any place on the earth's surface. It uses a pair of numbers, like 53.489, 1.379, to designate a certain distance (measures in degrees) north or south of the equator and east or west of the prime meridian (which runs through Greenwich, London, UK). This is a very flexible system because it can represent any location across the earth, but it uses angular units (degrees), which makes measuring distances difficult because the size of a degree varies depending on where you are on the earth's surface. This system is a type of geographic coordinate system.

Another common system (when using data for Great Britain) is the British National Grid (EPSG: 27700). This was developed by the Ordnance Survey, and is the system used on the pink Landranger map series (among others), and what you may have learnt at school. There is a notional 0,0 location to the south west of the Isles of Scilly, and then each location is measured as a certain number of metres east of this (eastings) and then a certain number of metres north (northings). This system is quite flexible, because it uses metres, and so is very easy to calculate distances. However, it is limited in geographical scope to Great Britain (and does not include Northern Ireland). This is a type of projected coordinate system.

A hybrid system was developed, to combine the benefit of using metres with the flexibility to show data anywhere in the world. This is called Universal Transverse Mercator (UTM) and it is based on the Mercator projection. This splits the world into grids, and each grid has its own projected coordinate system in metres. You can use this system to represent data anywhere in the world, but you can't use it to represent data across a very large area. Each grid (or zone) is its own coordinate system (and therefore has its own EPSG code; see Figure 15).

The key bit about coordinate systems is that every spatial data set uses a coordinate system, and when we use data from more than one system, we need to reproject the data (change the data from one coordinate system to another). Most GIS will automatically reproject the data for us. However, sometimes the software gets this wrong, so we have to intervene. Often the cause of this is that the GIS doesn't know what coordinate system the data are in, in which case it will ask the user. This then relies on the user knowing what coordinate system the data are in. Additionally, sometimes the coordinate system information in a spatial data file can get corrupted or the GIS can get confused, and this is where we have to intervene.

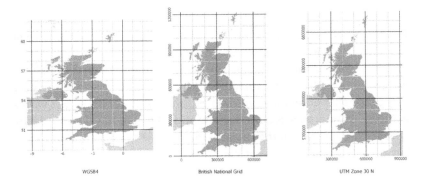

Figure 15 The UK represented using different coordinate systems. L to R: WGS84 (latitude / longitude), British National Grid, UTM Zone 30 N. *Map created by Nick Bearman using Ordnance Survey Boundary Line Data (UK outline) © Crown copyright 2020 and Natural Earth data (Other countries).*

Key signs that the data we are using are in the wrong coordinate system is when you load two sets of data for one geographic area, but they appear in different 'places' on the map. This is one of the key problems with spatial data, and can account for a significant proportion of the issues in any GIS project!

Files, databases and APIs

So far we have discussed how we conceptualize space and whether we store data as vector or raster. Given that our GIS is running on a computer, we have to store that data somehow on the computer.

The most common method of storing data is in a file, and by far the most common form of file for spatial data is a shapefile. Shapefiles are used for vector data, and have been around for many years (they were first introduced in the early 1990s). The fact they have been around for such a long time means that every GIS can read and write shapefiles, and they are a really useful way of exporting data from one program to another. However, they do have some restrictions and at times can be tricky to use.

Shapefiles are made up of (a minimum of) three different files, which are as follows:

- myshapefile.shp
- myshapefile.shx
- myshapefile.dbf
- *myshapefile.prj (optional)*

The .shp file is the key one – this is what we open in QGIS[3] (or whichever GIS you use) and it contains the coordinate information (the actual shapes of the spatial data). The .shx file is an index file, and the .dbf is the attribute table, or the spreadsheet that contains the attribute data of the shapefile. Sometimes you will get one (or more) other files with a shapefile – the .prj one is quite important, as this contains the coordinate system the data are in. If the .prj file is missing, the shapefile will still work, but the GIS won't know what coordinate system the data are in. It will ask us what coordinate system the data are in, and if we get this wrong, it can cause lots of problems later on. The key bit to know about shape files is that for them to work you need to move all of the files together.

---

[3] Previously QGIS was known as Quantum GIS, but now it is just known as QGIS.

If you just move the .shp file and not the others, it is a bit like having the members of a brass band, but without their music. The best approach is to either move the whole folder or, if you are emailing someone, zip all of the files together into a zip file, and then attach that to an email. If you are working with confidential or sensitive data, you may need to take extra security precautions.

While shapefiles are the most common, there is a whole selection of different file types. Another key one is geopackage, which is relatively new, but over the long term may well take over from shapefile, as it is a much more flexible format. One big benefit is that everything is stored in one file, and it also removes many of the other limitations of the shapefile format.

With shapefiles and geopackages being used for vector data, we have a different range of options for raster data. One of the most common ones is TIFF which is a standard image format. Raster data is a gridded data set, exactly the same as an image, so many of the formats are the same. Sometimes a TIFF is referred to as a GeoTIFF when the image comes with a set of coordinates that allows a GIS to load the image and show it in the correct geographic location. Another common format is ASCII GRID, which stores raster data in a plain text file, something you can open it in Notepad.

Along with files, it is also possible to store spatial data in a database. This is very common when you are sharing data between many different users and want to store the data in a central location. There are many different types of databases and nearly all of them use an SQL-based language to access the data (e.g. SELECT * FROM table;). One of the most common ones is Postgres, and it has a special extension called PostGIS that allows it to handle spatial data. This not only allows us to store spatial data, but also runs spatial queries (e.g. SELECT * WITHIN 10 miles of x,y FROM table;). GeoPackage gets a special mention here, as it is really a database stored within a file. This means it has all of the advantages of databases, plus all of the benefits of being stored in one file.

Application Programming Interfaces (APIs) are another way of accessing data. Instead of having the file on your computer, or accessing a database on a server, you can connect to an API across the internet and access the data as you need it. This has the benefit of the data always being up to date and in some cases it will automatically style and resize the data ready for your map. Some APIs provide data for free, and some charge.

With spatial data we have two different types of API. Web Mapping Service (WMS) provides spatial data as an image. This means we can view the data and use it as a base map, but we can't see the actual data underneath, or query it. The other type of API is Web Feature Service (WFS), which provides the spatial data as features, so we can actually see the data underneath, measure it and use it in mapping and analysis.

Which method to use?

With all of these choices, which ones should we use for our data? The vast majority of the time we don't actually get a choice at all, because we get the data from elsewhere, so we have to work with whatever format it is provided in. It is possible to convert data (from vector to raster or from shapefile to geopackage) but most of the time it is best not to convert the data unless you have a specific need to. If you are in the situation where you are creating new data and need to make decisions about how to store it, it is a good idea to find out what other people have done in similar situations and how they have stored similar data before.

However we choose to conceptualize our data (discrete objects or continuous fields), store it (vector or raster) or access it (file, database or API), we always have a series of limitations when using spatial data. We can store only so much information in our spatial data; it is a model of the world. As such, we have different models for different use, so we always need to ask: Are the data and the model that we are using appropriate for what we are trying to achieve? Does the data have enough detail, and does it have the attributes we need? We also need to think about whether our data is up to date, and is it at a suitable scale?

Summary

Spatial data is a key ingredient in our GIS and how we store this data has many practical implications. We need to know which projection and coordinate system our data set uses, particularly important for when we have to combine together data sets from multiple sources. We can conceptualize the world as discrete objects or a continuous field, and then use either vector data or raster data to represent this within our GIS. We also have a choice of different file types, including shapefiles, GeoPackages, GeoTIFFs and ASCII GRIDs.

6 Spatial data analysis

Chapter objectives

Spatial analysis can be anything from plotting data onto the map and looking at spatial patterns to advanced spatially based regression analyses. This chapter discusses a range of different spatial data analysis techniques and how they can be applied to social science as well as a range of spatial statistics that we can calculate and use to characterize our spatial data.

After reading this chapter you will:

- be aware of different types of spatial analysis,
- understand the value of descriptive maps as a method of spatial data representation,
- understand spatial autocorrelation and a range of spatial statistics,
- know how and when to apply spatial overlays in a range of situations and
- be aware of different types of spatial analysis.

Descriptive maps

GIS is a very flexible tool and can be used in many different ways. One of the simplest applications, but also a very powerful one, is to show data on a map. Just the very act of representing data in its spatial location can provide us with a huge amount of information.

For example, we might look at the distribution of a certain disease and surmise some information about how it spreads (e.g. John Snow's cholera, Chapter 1). We might also look at how the level of deprivation varies across space in a city and see how this relates to income, ethnicity or a range of other factors (see choropleth maps, Chapter 3).

This does not necessarily involve any explicit spatial analysis or calculations at this stage – we are solely looking at spatial patterns and combining what we see on the map with our knowledge of the local area. This is a very powerful tool and can be used in many, very effective ways.

Of course we can develop this much further and perform some spatial analysis to derive some more information from the spatial data we are using. We can split these into two groups – spatial statistics, which give us numerical information about the data, and spatial overlays, which allow us to perform multi-criteria decision analysis. Before moving on to spatial statistics, there are a couple of important concepts we need to consider – modifiable areal unit problem (MAUP) and the ecological fallacy.

MAUP and the ecological fallacy

MAUP

The MAUP is a key issue when dealing with grouped spatial data. Grouped spatial data might sound quite specific, but we come across it more often that you might think. Census data is a special type of grouped spatial data, and we may well end up using it a lot. We might also end up grouping data by local authority or LSOA for a wide variety of reasons – privacy, to minimize file size, to get an overview of data for an area or for comparison with other data sets. Electoral boundaries are also a key example of grouped data; in the UK, voters are grouped into constituencies and then voters within each constituency elect an MP. With all grouped data, the location of the groups is vitally important. If the same source data is grouped together differently, then you can get very different results. Constituency boundaries and voting are great examples of these. Figure 16 shows how even when the underlying data do not change, a change in the boundaries can create a very different result.

Voting data is a great example of how altering the boundaries can impact the result of who is elected. Altering the boundaries intentionally to create a certain result is called gerrymandering and can be quite common in Northern Ireland and the United States. MAUP is the formal name for this feature, and this stems from the fact that the Aerial Units (i.e. the areas we are grouping data by) are Modifiable (i.e. we can move the boundaries as we see fit). There is no one 'correct' set of boundaries – we are just artificially imposing them on the data. For more details, see Longley et al. (2010) and Openshaw (1984a, 1984b, 1981).

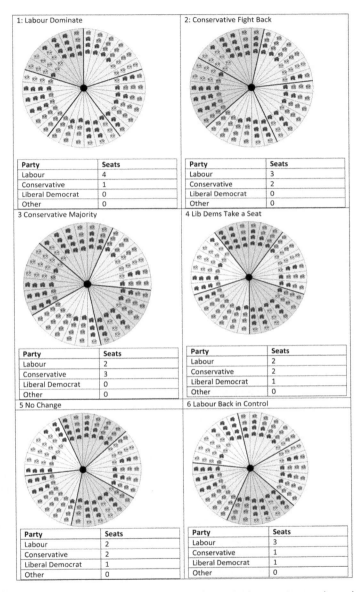

Party	Seats		Party	Seats
1: Labour Dominate			**2: Conservative Fight Back**	
Labour	4		Labour	3
Conservative	1		Conservative	2
Liberal Democrat	0		Liberal Democrat	0
Other	0		Other	0
3 Conservative Majority			**4 Lib Dems Take a Seat**	
Labour	2		Labour	2
Conservative	3		Conservative	2
Liberal Democrat	0		Liberal Democrat	1
Other	0		Other	0
5 No Change			**6 Labour Back in Control**	
Labour	2		Labour	3
Conservative	2		Conservative	1
Liberal Democrat	1		Liberal Democrat	1
Other	0		Other	0

Figure 16 'Gerrymander City' showing how a change in the constituency boundaries, without any change in individuals' votes, can change the outcome of the election and which party is in power. *Based on https://twitter.com/DrBobBarr/status/11963588 15748370432, credit: ERS (Electoral Reform Society), Geoff Powell and Proportional Representation Society of Australia.*

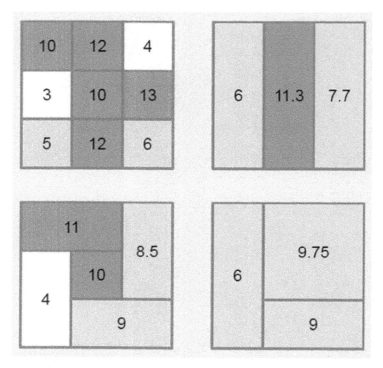

Figure 17 The impact on grouping data together in different ways, calculating the average value of the cells, with the original source data (top left).

Figure 17 shows different ways of grouping data together. We have the original source data in the top left, and then three different ways of grouping it together. See how the values vary when the data are grouping together differently. However, when we are working with grouped data, we won't have access to the original source data, and we won't know which of the possible groupings has been used.

While this is an issue with all data, MAUP is taken into account with Census data. MAUP is a well-known geographical phenomena, and the Office of National Statistics (ONS), in conjunction with academics at the University of Southampton, developed a method to group Census data according to certain criteria (Cockings et al., 2011; Martin, 2004, 1992; Martin et al., 2001). Their criteria were, within the requirements from the Census (of each output area having about 100 households within it), to make the areas as homogeneous as possible. This would then minimize the impact of MAUP because we have a justification for this allocation of boundaries, as opposed to any other. It is not possible to remove the impact of MAUP completely, and whenever working with grouped data, we need to remember this.

Ecological fallacy

The ecological fallacy is a similar (but slightly different) issue to the MAUP. The ecological fallacy is making the assumption that everyone in one geographic unit has the same characteristics. For example, we might have an area that overall has a relatively high level of deprivation. However, each individual within this area will have different levels of deprivation, and it would be wrong to assume that everyone in this area is deprived. It is exactly the same issue as using an average to summarize a group of statistics – the average can tell us a lot, but it won't tell us anything about the statistical outliers.

Another term that is related is the individualistic fallacy – this is the inverse of the ecological fallacy, and this is when we assume that every individual has their own deprivation level, and are not impacted by the deprivation around them. Like most aspects of geography, it is a combination, and while the individual's deprivation is important, it is also impacted by the area's deprivation.

Spatial statistics

Statistics gives us a huge range of options to compare data sets, helps us decide whether there are significant differences and helps us to establish whether our sample is representative of the wider population. We can apply many of the same statistics to spatial data, and we also have a much wider range of statistical tests and analyses we can perform. A group of these are closely tied to the concept of space, and key to this is spatial autocorrelation. This is a measure of how important space (and spatial distribution) is in the location of distribution of a variable across space.

This statistic can tell us whether data are randomly spread across space, or whether space is influencing their location. This is a Moran's I statistic, and much like a R^2 value in a standard correlation, spatial autocorrelation varies between +1 and −1. A value of +1 means the data are positively spatially autocorrelated and that space has a very strong positive influence on their location, which results in all of the high values next to each other

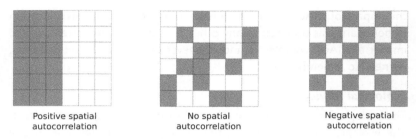

| Positive spatial autocorrelation | No spatial autocorrelation | Negative spatial autocorrelation |

Figure 18 (a) Positive spatial autocorrelation, (b) no spatial autocorrelation and (c) negative spatial autocorrelation.

and all of the low values next to each other (see Figure 18a). A value of -1 means the data is negatively spatially autocorrelated and that space has a very strong negative influence on their location, which results in data being spread equally across the data set (see Figure 18c). A value of around 0 represents the fact that space has no influence on their location, and so the data are distributed at random (see Figure 18b). Much like R^2 values, it is rare to get a value of +1.0 or −1.0 in real-world data, and values between +0.5 and −0.5 are much more common. We would use this type of analysis to measure how important the spatial distribution of a particular variable was, and it would show whether the variable was distributed across space at random, or whether there was some spatial clustering, that is, whether something was making higher values and lower values cluster together beyond a random distribution.

Deprivation is often something that is measured using a variety of different methods, and often used as an example when looking at spatial autocorrelation, because deprivation is usually not distributed at random. There are often other underlying factors that vary with space that influences deprivation, and therefore spatial autocorrelation is seen in the deprivation. Ferguslie Park, Paisley (west of Glasgow, Scotland, UK), has been recorded as the most deprived area in Scotland in one of the earlier measures of this type in the 1970s, and in the 2016 version of the IMD (Crow et al., 2019). Equally, it also highlights the impact of the ecological fallacy, as deprivation is highly variable within Ferguslie Park as well (see Figure 19).

We also have a measure called local indicators of spatial association (LISA) which allows us to measure the spatial clustering of the data – that is, are there more cases in this location than we would expect in a randomized

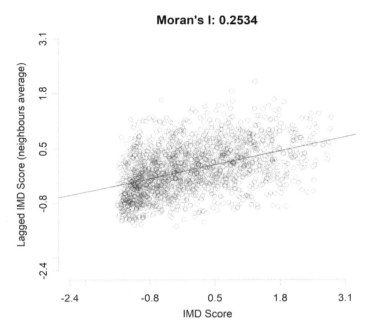

Figure 19 An example of a Moran's I output, showing the spatial autocorrelation of IMD (Index of Multiple Deprivation, 2015) scores (high = highly deprived, low = low levels of deprivation) for Manchester, UK. *Contains National Statistics data © Crown copyright and database right (2020). Contains OS data © Crown copyright (2020).*

distribution? This analysis provides us with a wide range of information and it can tell us whether we have clusters of higher or lower values, where these clusters are and how significantly different these clusters are. This would be able to tell us where these clusters of higher or lower values were located (see Figure 20).

The final type of spatial statistics I am going to mention here is geographically weighted regression (GWR). This is an exploratory method that develops a standard regression model to explicitly model the impact of space in the relationship of data that we are modelling. It works by running a regression model at each separate spatial location, and then comparing these models across the whole data set. It will tell us how the regression relationship varies across space, and which regression variables stay the same across space (spatial stationarity) and which vary (spatial non-stationarity). This will allow us to start to work out which factors might be

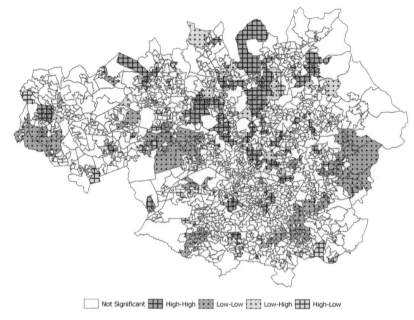

Not Significant ⊞ High-High ▦ Low-Low ⦂ Low-High ⊞ High-Low

Figure 20 An example of a LISA (Local Indicators of Spatial Association) output. L shows the significance level of the clustering, and R shows the type of cluster (whether high values are surrounded by high values, high values surrounded by low values, etc.). The data shown here is IMD (Index of Multiple Deprivation, 2015) scores (high = highly deprived, low = low levels of deprivation) for Manchester, UK. *Contains National Statistics data © Crown copyright and database right (2020). Contains OS data © Crown copyright (2020).*

driving the spatial variation we are seeing. We can run these statistical tests in a variety of different software packages, probably the easiest to use is GeoDa; see Chapter 8 for more details on GeoDa (see Figure 21).

Spatial overlays

The second area of spatial data analysis is a set of tools called spatial overlays or spatial intersections. This allows us to relate different layers of spatial information together and to ask questions like 'which areas are within a certain distance from this feature, and also beyond a certain distance from this other feature?' These include tools like buffers, unions, clips and point in polygon analysis. Often these are a key element of any multi-criteria

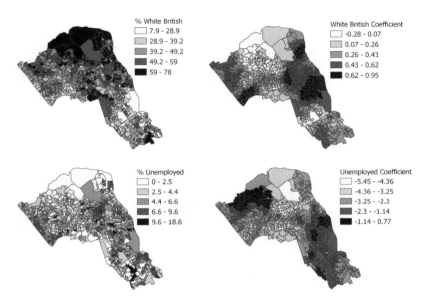

Figure 21 An example of an output from a geographically weighted regression (GWR) analysis. It shows the proportion of residents who identify as white British (top left) and who are unemployed (bottom left) and the regression coefficient for each of these (top right and bottom right, respectively). *Contains National Statistics data © Crown copyright and database right (2020). Contains OS data © Crown copyright (2020).*

decision analysis, where we use GIS to find a geographic area that meets a range of criteria.

A good example of a multi-criteria decision analysis is a site selection for a new water pipeline. We will have a series of criteria, for example, to be within 2 km of a main road, to ensure easy access for construction and maintenance. We might also need to be more than 600 m away from a river, to minimize risks related to land movement and more than 1 km from areas of tribal forest, to minimize impact on the indigenous tribal population. We might also have a slightly more complex calculation, saying we don't want the height of the land to be more than 100 m, to minimize the construction cost and the need for pumping. All of this can be achieved with a range of tools within GIS.

Buffers are one of the most used tools of spatial data analysis. This allows us to draw an area around a spatial object at a set distance. For example, if we had a 500 m buffer around a point, we would draw a circle with a

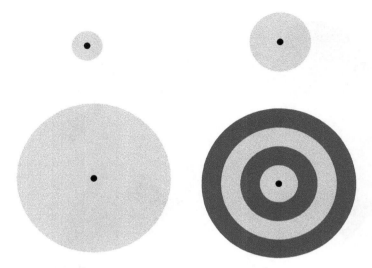

Figure 22 A series of points, with buffers around them. Top left: 100 m buffer, top right: 200 m buffer, bottom left: 500 m buffer, bottom right: a 'multiring' buffer, with buffers at intervals of 125 m.

500 m radius around the point (or each point) in our data set. This can also be extended to any line or polygon feature, or any layer of features (see Figure 22).

The clip tool allows us to select out areas of spatial data, using a 'cookie-cutter' type approach. For example we might clip out an area of a buffer. The dissolve tool combines areas together that are the same, or have the same characteristics. The intersection tool splits data up (see Figure 23).

Most frequently these overlay tools are used in combination. For our water pipeline example, we might use an approach like the one shown in Figure 24.

Spatial analysis

There are also other spatial analysis tools that are useful in different circumstances. Point in polygon is a very useful analysis that allows us to count how many points are within each polygon. For example, if we had a series of crime data as points and we wanted to see how many crimes

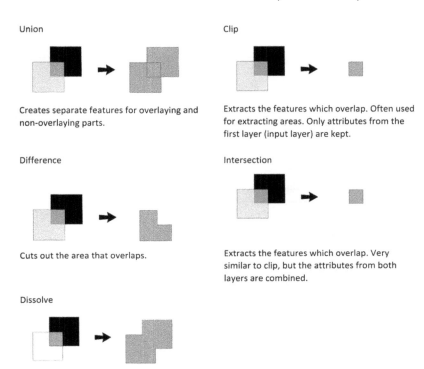

Figure 23 A series of different overlay operations common in GIS.

occurred in each LSOA (a polygon data set) then we could use point in polygon analysis to do this. Nearest-neighbour analysis can be used to work out which service (such as a shop or doctor's surgery) is closest to each house within a certain area. This could then be used to work out how easily different people can access certain services.

This is just a very small selection of GIS tools that are available. Most GIS analyses involved a selection of different GIS tools, combined together to analyse the data in whichever way is required.

Summary

Spatial data analysis provides us with a wide variety of tools to ask questions of our spatial data. We can do this in a range of different ways, from creating

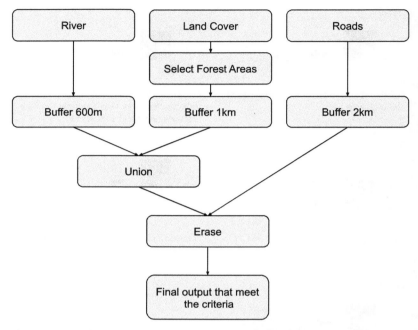

Figure 24 Flowchart showing the data and geo-processing tools used in a multi-criteria decision analysis for routing a new water pipeline.

descriptive maps to give us powerful insights to performing spatial overlays providing us with the ability to ask 'where' questions. We also have a range of spatial analysis techniques which give us the tools to perform spatially based statistical analysis on our data.

7 GIS software

Chapter objectives

There are many different types of software we can use to work with spatial data, with different ones appropriate in different fields of study or for different works. This chapter will give you an overview of the different types of software and the main pros and cons of them. It will also link to some tutorials for the main pieces of GIS software.

After reading this chapter you will:

- understand the different types of GIS software available,
- be aware of closed-source and open-source software and how they are different,
- be able to find out more information about different types of GIS software,
- be aware of the main advantages and disadvantages of each type of GIS software, and
- know where to find more information and tutorials on different types of GIS software.

There is a huge range of GIS software available. There is no one 'right' piece of software which is best depends on the data you have and what you are trying to do with it. Different types of software have different advantages and disadvantages, and you will often end up using multiple pieces of GIS software for a particular project – this is perfectly normal (this is also why good file management is important to ensure you are working on the correct files, see Chapter 8). The 'best' piece of software for a specific job also depends on you and the ways in which you like to work.

This chapter splits GIS software into the following three categories:

- Web Mapping
- Desktop GIS: ArcGIS and QGIS
- Coding GIS: R and Python

Types of GIS software

One of the biggest differences is whether you use a graphic interface or a command-based interface. If you have ever used a Stata Do file, then this is a command line–based interface. This is where you run your analysis using a series of text-based commands, rather than clicking and selecting options from drop-down menus. If you dislike Stata Do files, then a graphic interface might be a better choice. It also depends on what you are trying to do – for example, a command-based interface allows you to include loops, where you can replicate a map for many different variables – a very handy trick. If you've not yet tried a command line–based interface, it is worth trying out, as many people get on with it really well, and it has some clear advantages (more on these later).

Another key difference is whether the software is proprietary (closed source) or open source. Proprietary software (or commercial software) means you pay a fee to use and is designed and supported by a commercial company. It could also be described as 'closed-source' as you do not have access to the source code – that is, you cannot see how it works. For example, when a particular spatial statistic has been implemented, you cannot see how it is calculated.

Open source software is free at the point of use, you can download it from the internet and use it, for academic or commercial work, with no licence fee to pay. It is also 'open source' which means you can see the computer code that runs the software. For example, you can see exactly how the software engineers implemented the code to calculate that spatial statistic. Open source software is also very appropriate for academic research because it contributes to your research being reproducible. Reproducible research is the concept that another scientist, with similar knowledge to you, could come along and read your paper, and recreate the experiment you ran, run the same analysis and check that they get the same results out. It is important to be able to do this because findings may be controversial, and in such cases it is useful to be able to check whether any mistakes have been made in the research process. Open source software contributes to this by (a) being free (so anyone can use it, with no requirement to pay a licence fee or be in an institution that pays for the software) and (b) being open source, so the methods used within the software are transparent.

The need for open source software

Being able to see the source code of a product may not seem that useful. However, in areas that perform highly technical and complex analysis (e.g. GIS) this can be quite important. Pete Fisher conducted an analysis of how different GIS software performed a viewshed analysis – a fairly standard piece of GIS analysis. He compared seven different pieces of GIS software and only two programs produced exactly the same result, and these two were related programs (one was an improved interface that ran on top of the other one). All of the other results were slightly different. The differences were fairly minor, but all stemmed from the fact that the algorithms to calculate a viewshed analysis were calculated slightly differently. In addition, one piece of GIS software had a serious error in it, resulting in erroneous viewshed results. This was reported to the developers and fixed, but we don't know how much analysis was performed with this software which generated incorrect results (Fisher, 1993). More recently, similar issues have been identified with digital elevation model (DEM) viewshed analysis (Riggs and Dean, 2007) which shows this is still something that should concern us.

If we could see the source code, we could compare the processes involved, and find out what is causing these differences. As it was, Pete Fisher had to compare the outputs and derive (or guess) what was causing the differences. This is also a reminder not to blindly trust the output of GIS analysis – always check it against what you were expecting, and ask, does this make sense?

This section will talk about different types of GIS software, explaining the three different areas – web, desktop and coding – and the advantages and disadvantages of each. Chapter 8 includes information and references on where to find more information on how to use each type of GIS package.

Web mapping

Web mapping is one of the most well-used GIS tools in existence. Many people you know will have used web mapping services, perhaps without knowing it. Google Maps and Google Earth are the most well known of these, and when Google Earth was released in 2005, it revolutionized the public's perception of GIS. For people who work in GIS, it made it so much easier to explain what they do: GIS is a bit like Google Earth/Google Maps, except that it is much more powerful and allows you to edit the data and add your own data.

Using Google Maps (or City Mapper, or one of the many other services) is how most people come across web mapping services. Planning a route from A to B has been revolutionized with web maps, and the number of web-based services that use maps is increasing exponentially. A key element of it, and the reason it is so successful, is because of its ease of use and flexibility. The recent rapid growth of running and personal fitness apps and devices has also generated a whole new swathe of data and interfaces – for example, Strava allows you to record a GPS log of your run, view it on a Google Maps basemap, and compare your statistics with other runners.

These tools allow us to create an interactive web map showing data we are interested in. For example, if we have some data from the Armed Conflict Location and Event Data (ACLED) database we can plot this on a webmap, and then users can explore the map, zoom in and out and click on the data points for more information about that specific event (see Figure 25).

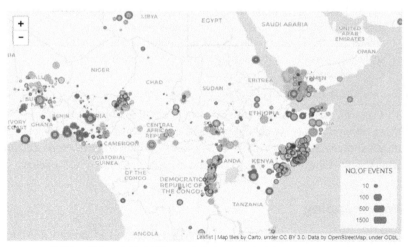

Figure 25 Example of an interactive web map, showing conflict data from ACLED for central Africa. *From Armed Conflict Location and Event Data Project (ACLED); https://www.acleddata.com.*

Some of the tools are also very flexible and allow us to customize the interface and include or exclude certain elements on the map. We could also allow the events on the map to be searched and allow users to select which type of events they want to show (e.g. violence against civilians, battles or riots/protests). This allows a greater level of flexibility on the website, and is beginning to bring traditional 'GIS' technologies into the web browser. Carto is a particularly good example of this; it provides a variety of web-based GIS analysis tools.

Google Maps is probably the most common web map, but there are many other services that can be used – MapBox, Carto, OpenStreetMap to name a few. Each has its own pros and cons, and there are always new products being launched. The majority of these services are commercial products, usually free for limited usage (e.g. 50,000 map views/month for MapBox[1]) and paid for options above this. This allows a great selection of tools with a huge variety of features to be available for many users at no cost.

There are also open source competitors (such as OpenStreetMap and OpenLayers). These pieces of software are all freely available, and you can install them on your own server. Most of them are also offered as hosted packages, where you pay for hosting and support. This makes it much easier to get up and running with these services.

Alongside these 'new' offerings, ArcGIS has its own online offering – ArcGIS Online. This provides an online interface that gives you some of the power of GIS within your web browser, such as viewing maps and some styling options. It also offers tight integration with ArcGIS Pro for more advanced analysis.

Desktop GIS: QGIS and ArcGIS

A desktop GIS is a piece of software that runs on your typical desktop or laptop computer. The name comes from the era when software used to be run on big, expensive mainframe computers (1970s and 1980s) and the fact that this new piece of software could be run on the computer on your desk was a novel thing. Like most computer software, Desktop GIS used to be quite restricted by the speed and power of the desktop computer it was running on. As computer hardware improved these limitations decreased

---

[1] https://www.mapbox.com/pricing/.

and by the early 2010s, GIS operations were more restricted by the software available than by the hardware performance.

There are several big names in the Desktop GIS industry, but ArcGIS (created by Esri) is the commercial leader and probably the biggest. Esri was founded by Jack and Laura Dangermond in 1969 as a land use consulting firm and was instrumental in developing one of the world's first commercial GIS products (Esri, 2019, 2015). Esri is something of a rarity in the world of big business, as it is not a public company, and still held privately by the Dangermonds. ARC/INFO (the forerunner to ArcGIS) was launched in 1982 and ever since the software has grown, now with a global presence. ArcMap (in some form) has been around since 1999, and version 10.8 came out in 2020. Esri is promoting a plan to migrate all of their users to a new product, ArcGIS Pro, so keep your eyes open for this as well.

If you are based at a university, often you will already have access to ArcGIS – check with your IT department or library. ArcGIS also provides a range of charity licences, so the software is available in the third sector. To buy a licence for commercial use for ArcGIS is a costly exercise – in the range of £1,500–£3,000 per user per year, so not a purchase to be undertaken lightly. Partly as a response to the dominance of ArcGIS and partly with shift to a focus on open source software, QGIS was developed as an alternative to commercial desktop GIS products, to allow a wider variety of users to access GIS tools. It is free and open source software (FOSS) and therefore free for anyone to use, for any purpose.

QGIS was originally released as Quantum GIS in 2002 and has regular updates from a vibrant community of contributors, and version 3.12 came out in 2020. Functionality is now at the level of its commercial competitors and many users in industry, public sector and academia are moving from ArcGIS to QGIS. QGIS is becoming more and more user friendly and easy-to-use 'out-of-the-box'. QGIS has a great community following and strong support from grass-roots users ('QGIS,' 2019).

If you want to start learning any desktop GIS, I would recommend either working through some tutorials online, or attending a short course. These will give you enough experience to understand what is going on behind the scenes in the software and help you troubleshoot when things go wrong. Being able to troubleshoot and solve these types of problems is key in any type of research and is something you can do readily. It might be in an unfamiliar environment, but the key steps are the same, so don't worry.

Coding GIS: R and Python

Working with spatial data in a GIS has typically used a graphical user interface (GUI) to work with the data and analysis. There are many advantages to using a code-based interface, or command line driven interface, including the ability to record scripts and repeat a set of analyses exactly at a later point, and to make use of computer programming concepts such as loops to easily allow the creation of multiple maps of similar design.

> One of the very early versions of Esri's GIS offering was command line driven (ARC/INFO) but when this was absorbed into ArcGIS Desktop, the command line approach was seen as a more advanced tool, with the GUI as the basic tool.

One of the major benefits of solely using a command line or scripting approach as a way of performing analysis is that every process and piece of analysis you do is recorded, so it is very easy to reproduce your analysis. This is useful in areas where you have frequent reports to run, such as a six-monthly report on activity. Once the six months are up, you just run the script again and get an updated output. It is also very handy if you have a series of variables to map for one area. You can make the first map, and then just repeat the code for the other variables – what is called a loop in computer science parlance (more on this later). In science it is very important for your research to be reproducible, and in some areas providing your script along with your source data allows any reader to re-run your analysis very easily.

One of the first widely used command line approaches to working with spatial data was the development of the spatial libraries for R. R was created in 1993, and was designed as an easily extendable programming language (Thieme, 2018). It was released as FOSS and the ease of adding extra commands (or libraries) was one of its keys to success. It allowed a whole variety of libraries to be developed, including a wide range of spatial libraries, which allow it to be used as a GIS (see Figure 26).

For a long time, R was primarily developed by computer scientists and statisticians. They made their work open and free for anyone to use. While the software was very useful, it wasn't particularly aesthetically pleasing software. RStudio was founded in 2008 by J. J. Allaire, who developed

Figure 26 RStudio, one of the main interfaces for working with the R language.

RStudio Desktop an integrated development environment (IDE) for R (RStudio, 2019). This makes it much easier to use R and manage the different elements you need to when writing R scripts. For anyone new to R, I would really recommend you use RStudio. They have some great resources (https://education.rstudio.com) and there are also many other tutorials and short courses available. RStudio (the company) has also contributed a whole range of other packages to the R environment, including a range of packages for data science (ggplot2, dplyr and tidyr), a great way of automating document creation including R code (R Markdown) and a great interface for creating interactive web graphics (Shiny).

Another very common language used with spatial data is Python. Originally developed in the late 1980s, Python is more of a traditional computer programming language than R, and so while being slightly trickier to write, it is more powerful and scalable than R. Python is designed as a general purpose language, to provide the setting to both experiment with new code and concepts easily and scale to large data sets/intensive pieces of analysis. Python is extendable, in a similar way to R, so there is a whole range of spatial Python libraries we can use. Some of these handle import and export, some different types of data analysis. Python is well used in the area of data science, and being able to use Python is a great employability skill and should not be turned down if you have the opportunity to learn it ('History of Python,' 2019).

In this area, like many others, different languages come and go depending on what is in 'vogue' at the time. Being able to code is a very valuable skill, particularly with the advent of big data, so if you have the opportunity of attending a workshop on R, Python or any other coding language, I would really recommend you take it up.

Summary

There is a very wide range of GIS software available to use, ranging from web-based GIS to desktop GIS and coding GIS. Which one is most appropriate depends on what you are trying to achieve and what output you want. You are likely to encounter all three during the course of your work and I would encourage everyone to spend some time trying all three, so that you are familiar with the differences. If you are not familiar with coding I would recommend spending some time learning R or Python, because with the increased use of these programs, coding is going to become a vital skill for researchers in all areas of the social sciences, not just the more technical areas of GIS.

8 Next steps

Chapter objectives

This chapter starts with considering the next steps for the area of GIS and how this is likely to change. Then it focuses on showing the reader the next steps, including options for 'learning by doing' using their own data in one of the software packages, making use of the tutorials available online. It will consider a variety of pieces of software and list some useful resources for each. It will also discuss the other options of online courses and in-person courses. The 'Focus on the data' section will highlight some useful data sources and discuss new and upcoming data sources and how they can be integrated into your GIS workflow.

After reading this chapter you will:

- know where to find resources for a range of different GIS software;
- understand why file management is important and how to implement a file management system,
- be able to use a range of troubleshooting techniques to solve problems when you encounter them and
- understand how to search for spatial data and evaluate whether it is appropriate for your project.

Next steps for GIS

The developments in technology and GIS have been very closely linked and will continue to be closely linked in the future. Most major technological developments in recent history (mobile phones, the internet, GPS, cloud computing) have had major impacts on GIS. While there will be many things that no one can predict, there are some upcoming developments that are likely to have a big impact on GIS.

Driverless vehicles are at the forefront of new technology, and data, including geographic data, will be underpinning them and their usage. This is both in terms of referencing themselves to the earth (using GPS/GNSS/other location technology) but also much more local spatial observation, whether it be through LiDAR, cameras or some other similar technology. Referencing all of this data to its location is vital to be able to navigate through this environment safely. 5G mobile data signals will play a big part of this, allowing this data to be communicated rapidly between cars and from the car to the car manufacturer and other interested parties. Whether they have the car owners'/users' consent to do this is a very different matter entirely and will also be something that has the potential to play a big role in the future of GIS.

Controlling travel without direct line of sight will have contributions to both end users (driverless cars) and also drones, used for data gathering and a whole other range of related uses. Not having direct line of sight makes the drone much more reliable on GIS data sets, and more importantly accurate and reliable GIS data sets. The area of artificial intelligence will also be very valuable to drones, and other geospatial technologies. Geospatial data will form a key part of these systems and they in turn will influence how GIS develops.

Geomatics and engineering often use many similar concepts to construct computer aided design (CAD) models and a whole range of modelling and GIS techniques in their work. GIS and CAD are very similar, but have never been truly integrated until the very recent development of building information management (BIM). BIM is a system that allows construction data about a building (e.g. materials used for walls, locations of pipes, electricity cables, etc.) to be stored in a standard format that is compatible with GIS. BIM, alongside the concept of Digital Twins, where sensors record a range of real-time data and this is incorporated into a digital model of a building to allow analysis of the condition of the building, is really pushing forward GIS and CAD integration and this will continue to develop.

Another area where we will see many developments that are related to GIS is in terms of how GIS is used. The barriers of entry to make use of GIS are lowering and it will become much more common for GIS to be used outside the traditional applications of geography, planning and regional studies. GIS is a very powerful tool and many more subject specialists will use it to more effectively understand and represent the data they work with.

Learning by doing

While you can learn a lot about GIS from books and the internet, I would really recommend you have a go with a GIS of your choice to see how it works. There are some great exercises available online (see links provided later in this chapter) and after completing some of these I would recommend you try loading your own data into the GIS. You learn a lot by trying different things and seeing what works. If you do attend a course, I would recommend you spend some time soon after the course (within a week or two) trying to apply the techniques you have learnt in the course to your own data sets. Some courses may even give you a little bit of time to do this while the instructor is there, and or one-to-one support afterwards. This will help you transfer the skills you have learnt from the course material onto working with your own data.

Web mapping

Google Maps and Google Earth

Google provides a range of tutorials for their software taking you through some of the more advanced features. My Maps is Google's tool to be able to customize and add your own data to their interface. Google Earth can be used to do some quite advanced customization with KML, HTML and JavaScript.

- Google Maps http://maps.google.co.uk/
- My Maps https://www.google.com/maps
- Google Earth http://earth.google.com/

  - Basic usage https://www.google.com/earth/education/
  - Advanced usage (KML/HTML) https://developers.google.com/kml/faq#getting-started

Mapbox

MapBox is one of the commercial competitors to Google Maps that allows users enormous flexibility to customize their base maps and add customized data on top.

- MapBox https://www.mapbox.com/
- Tutorials https://docs.mapbox.com/studio-manual/help/

Leaflet

Leaflet is an open source, customizable JavaScript mapping library. It is as customizable as MapBox (probably more) but more technical to implement. On the other hand, it is open source, so it is free for anyone to use.

- Leaflet https://leafletjs.com/
- Quick Start Examples https://leafletjs.com/examples/quick-start/

OpenLayers

OpenLayers is similar to Leaflet, in that it is an open source, customized JavaScript mapping library. It can do much more than Leaflet, but is also much larger and more complex to use.

- OpenLayers https://openlayers.org/
- Examples https://openlayers.org/en/latest/examples/

Carto

Carto is one of the newer commercial offerings that go beyond the cartographic options offered by products like MapBox and offer some spatial analysis tools as well. They offer some of their tools for free and if you are working with a small, non-commercial project, many of their tools are free.

- Carto https://carto.com/

ArcGIS Online

ArcGIS Online is the online offering from Esri and couples very tightly with their ArcGIS Pro desktop software. The map design and analysis aspects are limited, but the interface is quite easy to use. It also allows for provision to publish your map online, so other people can access it.

- ArcGIS Online https://www.arcgis.com/
- Using ArcGIS Online https://learn.arcgis.com/en/paths/try-arcgis-online/

OpenStreetMap

OpenStreetMap is more a data source than a mapping library. In some ways it is similar to Google Maps in terms of what it does, but the data is completely open source, so anyone can use it for any purpose. For the interface, it uses Leaflet in fact.

- OpenStreetMap https://www.openstreetmap.org/
- OSM Data can be downloaded from a variety of sources (go under 'Export') but I would suggest https://download.geofabrik.de/

Desktop GIS

QGIS

QGIS is the leading open source desktop GIS program and is used by a wide variety of commercial, not-for-profit and local and national government organizations. The software is available from www.qgis.org and they also have some training material available, as well as a full user manual. There are numerous free training materials online, as well as some in-person courses. A variety of companies also offer commercial support packages.

- QGIS https://qgis.org/
- Training Manual https://docs.qgis.org/3.10/en/docs/training_manual/index.html
- *Learning QGIS: Create Great Maps and Perform Geoprocessing Tasks with Ease* is a great book written by Anita Graser (2018).

Esri ArcGIS

ArcGIS has been the leading commercial GIS software for twenty years, probably a lot longer. They offer very good access for academics (most universities have access to the software) and larger charities can apply for free or reduced cost access. A commercial licence is very expensive (costs approximately £1,500–£3,000 per user per year) and can usually be justified only by larger consultancies.

ArcGIS is a package (much like Microsoft Office) with a number of programs within it include ArcMap (the main program, for GIS data editing, map design and analysis), ArcCatalog (for spatial file management), ArcScene (for 3D work) and a range of other tools. They also have a range of extensions available (e.g. Spatial Analyst or Network Analyst) which make additional tools available for a further cost.

Recently Esri have launched ArcGIS Pro (ArcGIS Professional), a completely revamped package that links much more tightly with ArcGIS

Online. Currently about two thirds of the analysis tools available in ArcMap have been migrated to ArcGIS Pro, and the long-term plan is to migrate all the tools over, and migrate all users to ArcGIS Pro. ArcGIS Pro has a much cleaner interface, and is much easier to use, particularly for those new to GIS.

Esri offer a range of training programs from their online campus and in-person training courses as well. Training is also offered by third-party companies, both online and in-person.

- ArcGIS https://www.arcgis.com/
- ArcGIS to ArcGIS Pro https://pro.arcgis.com/en/pro-app/get-started/migrate-to-arcgis-pro.htm
- Esri Training https://www.esri.com/training/

GeoDa

GeoDa is a type of desktop GIS, but one that specializes in spatial analysis. It allows you to do interactive spatial analysis and provides a wide variety of spatial analysis tools, including spatial autocorrelation/Moran's I and Local Indicators of Spatial Association. It also is one of the few GIS programs that very effectively implements brushing or linked displays. For example, when you have a map open and highlight certain areas on the map, the same areas will be highlighted on any other graphs, histograms, scatter plots or tables you have opened.

GeoDa is a free and open source piece of software. It was created by Luc Anselin and his team (Anselin, 2006). Anselin also gives lectures on a variety of spatial analysis techniques, and some of these have been filmed and are available on YouTube.

- GeoDa http://geodacenter.github.io/
- Workbooks http://geodacenter.github.io/documentation.html
- Anselin lectures on YouTube https://bit.ly/30Etett

Coding GIS

R

R is one of the big newcomers to GIS. It is a scripting language, so works in a very different way to typical graphical user interface (GUI) GIS programs like QGIS or ArcMap. R is an open source program, so while there is a central repository for the software and associated libraries, there is no central provision for training material. RStudio works as an environment on top of R, and I would really recommend using RStudio when working with R code.

Libraries can be written by anyone and allow R to perform different analysis or work with different types of data. SP (SPatial) is the original spatial library, and this is in the process of being replaced by SF (Simple Features). Some training material will use SP, some SF and some will use both. Any good training material will explain the difference between the two and when you will likely come across them.

There are several mapping visualization libraries (such as tmap and ggplot) which allow for easier mapping of spatial data. They each have their pros and cons and some material will focus on one or the other.

- Download R https://cran.r-project.org/
- Download RStudio https://rstudio.com/

Python

Python has had some recent developments in the spatial area as well. It is a programming language, broadly similar to R (so very different to QGIS) but probably more of a proper programming language than R (although don't say that to programmers – in their view, it is still a scripting language and not a 'proper programming language' like C++!) Python works better with larger data sets than R and is usually more efficient.

Again, Python is open source and while there is a central location for the code, there is no central resource of training materials. Anaconda is a commonly used interface for Python. A range of more complex analyses can be done in Python, although it is very rarely used for direct GIS output. Most often Python outputs are loaded into R, QGIS or something else for visualization.

- Python https://www.python.org/
- Anaconda https://www.anaconda.com/distribution/

File management

Whatever type of GIS you use, you will end up creating a lot of files with it. It is vitally important you spend some time thinking about file management. We discussed the different types of spatial data files in Chapter 5, but whichever method you choose to use, you are going to end up with a lot of files. One thing everyone needs to do is to spend some time understanding where your GIS program stores data files, what files it stores and what is stored in each file.

QGIS is a great example; it works like most other desktop GIS in that it has project files. QGIS project files have the extension (the bit of the file name after the ".") of QGZ. This is what you save when you click Project > Save in QGIS. The vital thing to know is that this does not contain any geospatial data. These are stored in different files, whether they are shapefiles, geopackages or something else. The project file contains links to each of the data files, and information on how they are symbolized, what order they are in the layers window and any map layouts you have created. Good practice is also to have a versioning system of these, in case either you make a mistake and need to go back to an earlier version or the file gets corrupted by the program and you need to go back. There are many ways of achieving this. I use a simple, manual system, by whenever I open the file and do some work on it, I save the project file as a new file with an incremental version number. For example:

- ch4-context-map-v1-NB.qgz
- ch4-context-map-v2-NB.qgz
- ch4-context-map-v3-NB.qgz

This will give you a good file history and allow you to easily go back to a previous version (see Figure 27). This technique is also useful for image outputs and even data, if you are editing data a lot. ArcGIS calls these files Map Documents, and they have the extension MXD. Another approach for versioning is to use a version control system, like Git. Git is a really flexible system and can be used in many areas. It is beyond this book, but I would recommend attending a course, or having a look at http://swcarpentry. github.io/git-novice/ for more details.

For a small project, you can potentially store all of your files in one folder for that project. This will keep all of the related files together and allow you to back them up easily, or zip them up and send to a colleague. However, if you start creating more than maybe twenty to thirty files, you will probably need some subfolders. If you are working on your own, then a series of subfolders to split the files into different types will work. For example:

- \mapfiles which would contain all of the project files
- \data which would contain all of the spatial data, and could have subfolders within it if needed

Figure 27 One thing never to do is to use the word 'final' in any file name, ever. This guarantees that whoever you have created the file for (supervisor, client, colleague) will come back with something they want you to change and then you will have to call your file FINAL-2 or FINAL-FINAL or something equally confusing! *'Piled Higher and Deeper' by Jorge Cham www.phdcomics.com.*

- \tables for all of the non-spatial data
- \images for maps output from map composer, or other graphs
- \documents (or \writing) for your written work

This is a very flexible setup which can be adapted to your needs. If you are working as a part of a larger a team, a more formal structure will probably be required. What is vital is that everyone working on the project is aware of what the structure is, how it works and where they should save different types of file (see Table 1).

Different companies might use different approaches but when working with a group of people (or even just one other person) the key element is to make sure you discuss how you are going to do this early on. It is

Table 1 A Possible Folder Structure to Aid with File Management

Folder name	Purpose	Read only or read-write
00_Data_ management	To store a list of all data sets used, including detail of where the data came from, licences associated with data and restrictions	Read only
01_Incoming_ Data	Store all data used in separate folders named with the convention SOURCE_ YYYYMMDD_DESCRIPTION	Read only *So the data is never edited or changed and you always have a copy of the data you originally received*
02_Work_In_ Progress	Stores a copy of work currently in progress, with subfolders: • 021_Documents • 022_Figures • 023_MXDs • 024_Processing	Read/write
03_Shared	When shared internally with a colleague, copy 02_Work_in_ progress to this folder, with a date and the associated subfolders	Read only
04_Issued	When work is shared with the client, store here in a folder named YYYYMMDD-DESCRIPTION	Read only
05_General_ Resources	Other information, such as logos and template	Read/write

very difficult to implement a file management procedure onto an existing project, with files already stored in some other system, or even with no system!

As well as understanding your file system, you should also take regular backups of your data. Ideally you should have at least three copies of your files, in two separate physical locations. This means that if your laptop gets stolen, or your office burns down, you can still access a relatively recent copy of your files. You also need to test your backups to make sure the system is working as you think it is. This is to avoid the situation where the loss or corruption of your files is compounded by discovering your most recent working backup is six months old.

Troubleshooting

Whatever work you are doing with spatial data, I guarantee that you will have a problem or issue with your GIS at some point. The skill of interpreting error messages and troubleshooting what has gone wrong with your GIS is a key one and something you will get a lot of practice at.

Whichever piece of GIS software you are using, some of the things you are likely to get at some point are error messages. Sometimes these can be quite useful and will tell you where the problem is and what you need to do to solve it. However, most of the time these error messages will not be that descriptive, and it will either say something that means nothing to you or be a 'general error message'. One of the best ones of these is in ArcGIS and is error 999999: 'Something unexpected caused the tool to fail.' This provides no information at all!

A good technique when getting error messages is firstly to double check the inputs, whether that be spatial data or parameters that you have specified. Another approach, particularly if you are using a Processing/ArcToolbox tool or a complex process and are getting really weird error messages, is the classic IT approach of turn it off and turn it on again. Save your work and restart the GIS program, often this can solve some problems.

Failing that, the next step is to google the error message. Nearly every problem you will encounter in a GIS someone else has had before, and there are thousands of these types of posts on the internet, most of which are on a website called Stack Exchange. This is a site where people post questions, and other people can post answers. Nearly every problem I have encountered is listed on Stack Exchange and each problem usually has a solution. It's rare to find a problem that is not on Stack Exchange, but if you do you can always post the problem you have on there. Remember to read the advice beforehand, and if you can, post some sample data to illustrate the problem, as this makes it much easier for others to understand the problem and help solve it.

With your googling, you may also find a tutorial or other information about the work you are doing. If you are using a tool that is new to you, I would recommend spending some time working through a tutorial. This will help you understand what is going on and may well solve your problem. Working through the tutorial will also probably be quicker than trying to troubleshoot an error in an area you are unfamiliar with, despite your instinct telling you it will take longer.

The other potentially very useful resource is other people; friends or colleagues who use GIS regularly. These people can be very useful to talk things through with, help you understand error messages or just generally moan about how your GIS is not doing what it is supposed to. You will also be a very valuable resource for them and you can help them with error messages and act as a sounding board for the thing they can't work out.

The other thing that will be very useful is experience. The more GIS you do and the more problems you encounter, the more confident you will be at solving these problems. A colleague of mine once described getting these error messages as filling up an experience jar. The more experiences you have, the more you fill this jar, and the easier these error messages get to solve. I would really recommend trying to get as much experience as possible and while the first couple of problems may seem daunting, they will get easier in the future.

Focus on the data

Data is key to any GIS; a GIS without data is like a band of musicians without any music. When using data we also need to review it critically – is it useful and relevant for the work we want to do? This is both in terms of scale/ level of detail and in terms of timeliness (how up to date is it?). Table 2 is a list of commonly used data sets – this is not exhaustive by any means, but hopefully is a useful starting point.

Table 2 Useful Spatial Data Sources

Name	Description	URL
GADM	GADM is a spatial database of the location of the world's administrative areas (or boundaries) for use in GIS and similar software.	gadm.org
Natural Earth	Natural Earth is a public domain map data set available at 1:10 m, 1:50 m, and 1:110 million scales.	naturalearthdata. com
Free GIS data	A list of useful GIS data sources.	freegisdata.rtwilson. com
Ordnance Survey Open Data	Ordnance Survey provides a wide range of free data sets for Great Britain, including roads, rivers, height, buildings and postcodes.	ordnancesurvey.co.uk/ opendatadownload/ products.html
EDINA Digimap	Edina is a service for academic users and a very good source of data for the UK. Two specific collections are Digimap (Ordnance Survey map data) and UKBORDERS (boundary data sets and census look-up tables for the UK). Most collections require separate registration, and proof of student status (usually just an email from a .ac.uk account).	digimap.edina.ac.uk/
OpenStreetMap	OpenStreetMap is a community-created spatial database of the world. Data is open source so can be used for any academic or commercial purposes. Click on the Export tab to access.	openstreetmap.org

Key aspects to remember

Introduction

This is a quick recap of each chapter; if you want more details, have a look at the relevant chapter.

1. Using GIS in social science

GIS is used widely in the social sciences, with many different case studies. We discuss some of the limitations of GIS, as it is not universally useful and not every problem can be solved with GIS. We also touch on how computer and software development have been key to the adoption of GIS, including the launch of Google Earth. Overall GIS is an incredibly flexible tool with a very wide variety of applications. It can probably be applied in some way to the area you are working on, whether that be cities, planning, politics, history, archaeology or nearly any social science.

2. The history of GIS

The use of GIS has changed throughout its history and will continue to do so. For a significant period GIS was limited by the technology available, but now computer processing power is generally not a problem. Now the limits of GIS are mostly to do with data and our conceptual understanding of the issues involved. The technology we use with GIS will continue to change and while we can teach users now how to use R or Python, it is also vital to teach them how to learn new programming languages and techniques as they come along, as new languages and approaches are being developed all of the time.

3. Creating maps

When we are creating any type of map in our GIS, there are a whole range of data-related issues to consider. The list in this chapter is a good starting point for anyone new to making maps, highlighting what you need to think about. It is not exhaustive, and there are more design-related items in Chapter 4 'Cartography'. The more maps you create, the easier this process will be and the more options, designs and styles you will explore. There is no one 'right' design for a particular set of data; just some that are more or less appropriate. You need to critically look at the maps you design and think about why you are making the decisions you choose for the classification methods.

4. Cartography

Here are my top tips for better maps:

- For choropleth maps, don't use the default Equal Interval classification scheme; Jenks or Natural Breaks is usually a lot better.
- Depending on your data, potentially adjust the class intervals to round numbers, and remove any decimal places if they are not relevant.
- Use a colour palette from Color Brewer.
- Remember some people are colour blind, and avoid red-green colour scales.
- Check the legend; are all the symbols on the map in the legend, and all the symbols in the legend on the map?

- Print the map out and proof a physical copy.
- Get a second opinion on the map layout.

5. *How is spatial data structured?*

Spatial data is a key ingredient in our GIS, and how we store this data has many practical implications. We need to know which projection and coordinate system our data set uses, particularly important for when we have to combine together data sets from multiple sources. We can conceptualize the world as discrete objects or a continuous field, and then use either vector data or raster data to represent this within our GIS. We also have a choice of different file types, including shapefiles, GeoPackages, GeoTIFFs and ASCII GRIDs.

6. *Spatial data analysis*

Spatial data analysis provides us with a wide variety of tools to ask questions of our spatial data. We can do this in a range of different ways, from creating descriptive maps to give us powerful insights to performing spatial overlays providing us with the ability to ask 'where' questions. We also have a range of spatial analysis techniques which give us the tools to perform spatially based statistical analysis on our data.

7. *GIS software*

There is a wide range of GIS software packages available to use, ranging from web-based GIS to desktop GIS and coding GIS. Which one is most appropriate depends on what you are trying to achieve and what output you want. You are likely to encounter all three during the course of your work and I would encourage everyone to spend some time trying all three, so you are familiar with the differences. If you are not familiar with coding I would really recommend spending some time learning R or Python, because with the increased use of these technologies coding is going to become a vital skill for researchers in all areas of the social sciences, not just the more technical areas of GIS.

8. *Next steps*

Some final key things to remember are as follows:

- GIS is used widely and applicable to nearly all social science areas.
- GIS used to be limited by the available technology, now we have the technology to do whatever we like with GIS, the limit is our imagination.

- There are many different ways of creating a map, and no one design is 'right' – it depends on what the map is for. There are some good rules of thumb to create a good map.
- Map design (cartography) can make a good map look amazing – don't skimp on this section as it will make your maps look much better.
- Spatial data is structured in a very different way to CSV files or Excel tables. Understand how your data is structured and you can save yourself a lot of confusion and wasted time.
- Spatial data analysis can answer many of the 'where' questions we have, and provide valuable insights into data that we wouldn't be able to get otherwise.
- There are many types of GIS software which are appropriate for different uses. Try several and see which one you like the best.
- Data is key to GIS, as is good file managed and knowing your troubleshooting techniques.

Glossary

Acknowledgements: Information required on any map, including copyright (e.g. for OpenStreetMap or Ordnance Survey Open Data) or other data sources

ArcCatalog: Part of the ArcGIS package, primarily used for managing spatial files such as shapefiles and personal geodatabases

ArcGIS: A commercial GIS software created by ESRI, consisting of ArcMap, ArcCatalog and ArcScene

ArcMap: Part of ArcGIS, the main program for creating and editing spatial data and maps

ArcScene: Part of ArcGIS, used for 3D data

Attribute table: The table of additional information associated with each shapefile (e.g. country names); access by right-clicking on the layer and selecting Open Attribute Table

BNG (British National Grid): A coordinate system used to represent locations in Great Britain, consisting of eastings and northings, for example, 603125, 112589 (see also UTM and WGS1984)

Buffer: A circle around a point, where the radius of the circle is the buffer distance

Cartography: The science and art of map making, the area that provides the skills and techniques to make a great map

Categorical: A variable that has a series of values with no inherent order, for example, country names, also known as nominal (see also variable type, quantitative)

Centroid: The centre point of a polygon

Choropleth: A type of mapping where different colours are used to represent difference values; can use categorical and ordinal data

Classes: The groups data are put into for a choropleth map

Classification: How the data are classified into different classes for a choropleth map (see also Jenks, equal count, equal interval and standard deviation)

Console window: It is where you can type in commands for R to run, clears whenever you reopen R or run more than 1,000 lines of commands see also scripts

Coordinate system: The type of coordinates that are used to represent a specific location (see also WGS1984, BNG and projection)

Coordinates: The numbers representing a specific location, usually presented in pairs (see also latitude, longitude, WGS1984, BNG and UTM)

Correlation: A measure of how much two variables are related, measured using a R^2 value

CSV (comma separated values): A standard format of tabular data, can be opened in Excel

CSVT: An optional file for use with CSV files which specifies the variable type of each column in the CSV file

Data frame (ArcMap): A section of the map in Layout View containing specific layers of spatial data

Data frame: A format of storing spatial and non-spatial data in R

Data type: How data is stored within the Attribute table, can be integer (whole numbers), real (decimal numbers) and string (text)

DEM (Digital Elevation Model): A raster representation of the height of the earth's surface

Eastings: A coordinate that specifies the distance east, in metres, from the coordinates 0,0 south-west of the Isles of Scilly (see also BNG and northings)

Environment: The area where the variables are stored, called Workspace by R, and can be shown by the command ls() can be saved

Equal count (Quantile): Classification method where data are split into a number of groups by putting the same number of data items into each group, also known as quantile, see also classification

Equal interval: Classification method where data are split into classes that are evenly distributed, for example, 0–20%, 21–40%, and so on, see also classification

Feature class: One layer within a personal geodatabase; can contain one of points, lines and polygons

Field calculator: Used to calculate new values (e.g. differences) from existing values for all rows in a vector layer, accessed from the Attribute table

Fisher: Classification method very similar to Jenks

Geodatabase: See personal geodatabase

Geographic Information Science (GIS): The development of the tools, software and processes used in Geographic Information Systems

Geographic Information Systems (GIS): Using spatial data to answer questions about our world (see also Geographic Information Science)

Geographic Coordinate System: Coordinate systems that cover the whole globe, such as latitude/longitude, also known as WGS 1984

GeoJSON: Vector spatial data file, consisting of points, lines and polygons; all saved in one file

GPS (Global Positioning System): A series of twenty-four satellites in orbit around the earth which allow a GPS device to locate itself, with an accuracy of 1 m to 10 m

History: Record of every command you have typed into R can be saved

Inset Map: A small map included on the main map to aid orientation, for example, a map of Ghana might include an inset map of Africa to show where Ghana is

Integer: A whole number used to represent data, can be used in a choropleth map (see also data type)

Jenks (natural breaks): Classification method based on the Jenks algorithm which groups similar data values together, also known as natural breaks, see also classification

Join: The process of linking two data frames (usually an attribute data frame and a spatial data frame by a common attribute or ID)

Joining: The process of linking attribute information to spatial data, often used so the information can be shown on a choropleth map

Latitude: A coordinate that specifies the distance north or south, ranging from 0° at the Equator to 90° (North or South) at the poles (see also WGS1984 and longitude)

Layers: When you add data into a GIS each different file appears as a different layer; this allows different data sets to be overlaid on one another (see also Table of contents and Layers window)

Layers window (QGIS): Panel on the left hand side of QGIS, showing the different GIS layers in your map; the order of the layers can be changed (known as the Table of contents in ArcMap)

Legend: An important part of any map, showing what the symbols or colours used on the map represent

Library: A set of commands that can be loaded and used in R (also known as package)

Lines: Used in vector data sets to indicate a linear feature, such as rivers, roads or railways; is a series of points joined together with lines

Longitude: A coordinate that specifies the distance east or west, ranging from 0° at the Prime Meridian to 180° (East or West) (see also WGS1984 and latitude)

MapInfo: A commercial GIS software, created by Pitney Bowes

MXD project file (.mxd) (ArcMap): A project file for ArcMap which contains links to all the data files, for example shapefiles or geodatabases) and information on how they are symbolised; the MXD file does not contain the data itself (see also QGIS project file)

Nominal: A variable that has a series of values with no inherent order, for example country names, also known as categorical (see also variable type, ordinal and quantitative)

North arrow: Used to show the direction of north on a map, used to aid orientation (see also inset map)

Northings: A coordinate that specifies the distance north, in metres, from the coordinates 0,0 south-west of the Isles of Scilly (see also BNG and eastings)

Ordinal: Similar to a categorical variable, but with a clear order, for example high priority, medium priority and low priority (see also variable type, quantitative)

Package: A set of commands that can be loaded and used in R (also known as library)

Personal geodatabase: A type vector of spatial data file, consisting of one or more feature classes; can only be used in ArcGIS (see also feature class)

Pixel: An individual unit in a raster data set, the size of the resolution squared (i.e. for a 100 m resolution raster data set, each pixel would be 100 m x 100 m, covering 10,000 square metres (or 1 hectare) of land)

Points: A vector data type used to indicate a specific location, such as sample collection points, bird nest sites, towns or cities

Polygons: A vector data type used to indicate areas, for example land parcels, counties and fields; is a series of points joined with lines and closed to indicate an area

Print composer: The tool in QGIS used to design maps and add a legend, scale bar, north arrow and any required acknowledgements or copyright

Projected Coordinate System: Coordinate system which covers a small area of the whole earth's surface, for example, British National Grid, which covers Great Britain

Projection: The way the sphere shaped earth is distorted to fit on a flat piece of paper (see also WGS1984, BNG and coordinate system)

QGIS: An open source GIS created as broadly similar to ArcMap which is free for anyone to download, use and improve

QGIS project file (.qgs) (QGIS): A project file for QGIS which contains links to all the data files (such as shapefiles and/or GeoJSON files) and information on how they are symbolised; the project file does not contain the data itself (see also MXD file)

Quantile (equal count): Classification method where data are split into a number of groups by putting the same number of data items into each group, also known as equal count, see also classification

Quantitative: A numeric variable with an inherent order, for example GDP per capita (see also variable type)

R: The main program used to run R commands, see also RStudio

R^2: The correlation coefficient of two different data sets, a value of 1 is a strong positive correlation, -1 is a strong negative correlation

Raster: A type of spatial data used with GIS, consisting of a regular grid of points spaced at a set distance (the resolution); often used to represent heights (DEM) or temperature data (see also vector)

Raster calculator: Used with raster data to calculate differences (subtract) or calculate other indices (e.g. NDVI)

Real: A decimal number used to represent data, can be used in a choropleth map (see also data type)

Resolution: The size of each pixel in a raster data set (e.g. 100 m, 1 km, 100 km) (see also pixel)

RStudio: An interface that runs on top of R, allowing easier management of variables, scripts and plots

Sat-nav: A navigation system in cars, which uses GPS to direct the driver to their destination

Scale: The ratio of units of distance on the map to units of distance in the real world; for example 1:25,000 means that 1 cm on the map represents 25,000 cm (or 250 m) in the real world; usually shown on a scale bar

Scale bar: Used to show the scale of a map

Script: A series of R commands that can be run on demand (filename usually ends with .R) useful for rerunning commands

Shapefile: A type vector of spatial data file, consisting of one of points, lines or polygons; represented in GIS as one file but in fact consisting of multiple files (between four and six files, with extensions of .shp, .dbf, .shx and .prj)

Spatial: Often used interchangeably with geospatial, although technically refers spatial or location techniques at any scale (e.g. the whole universe down to atoms), whereas geospatial refers to spatial or location techniques at human to planet scales

Standard deviation: Classification method based on standard deviation and mean of the data set

String: A piece of text (e.g. a name) used to represent data, cannot be used in a choropleth map (see also data type, real and integer)

Style (QGIS) / Symbology (ArcMap): The options to choose the colours and/or symbols to represent data on the map; accessed through right-clicking on the layer and selecting properties and navigating to the Style tab)

Table of contents (ArcMap): Panel on the left hand side of ArcMap, showing the different GIS layers in your map; the order of the layers can be changed (known as the Layers window in QGIS)

Tabular data: Data laid out in rows and columns, as used in Excel (see also CSV)

UTM (Universal Transverse Mercator): A type of coordinate system used to represent any location in the world, consisting of a series of zones and a set of coordinates for each zone, in metres (see also BNG and WGS1984)

Variable: The way R stores values and data, assigned using the <- command

Variable type: Information on the type of information within a variable, can be categorical, ordinal or nominal

Vector: A type of spatial data used with GIS, consisting of points, lines and polygons (see also raster)

Vertex (vertices): Name for each of the points that connect the line segments of a line or polygon shapefile

WGS1984: A coordinate system used to represent any location in the world, consisting of latitude and longitude, for example 51.0426 N, 1.3772 E or 51.2° 33.53' N, 1.22° 38.23' E (see also BNG and UTM)

Workspace: The area where the variables are stored, called Environment by RStudio and shown in the top right hand corner

References

Allen, A., Lambert, R., Apsan Frediani, A., Ome, T., 2015. Can Participatory Mapping Activate Spatial and Political Practices? Mapping Popular Resistance and Dwelling Practices in Bogotá Eastern Hills. *Area* 47, 261–71. https://doi.org/10.1111/area.12187

Anselin, 2006. GeoDa: An Introduction to Spatial Data Analysis. *Geographical Analysis* 38, 5–22.

Battersby, S.E., Finn, M.P., Usery, E.L., Yamamoto, K.H., 2014. Implications of Web Mercator and Its Use in Online Mapping. *Cartographica* 49, 85–101. https://doi.org/10.3138/carto.49.2.2313

Big Mac Index, 2019. Wikipedia, https://en.wikipedia.org/wiki/Big_Mac_Index (accessed 22 July 2020).

Brewer, C., 2019. ColorBrewer [WWW Document]. URL http://www.ColorBrewer.org (accessed 15 November 2019).

Cockings, S., Harfoot, A., Martin, D., Hornby, D., 2011. Maintaining Existing Zoning Systems using Automated Zone-Design Techniques: Methods For Creating the 2011 Census Output Geographies for England and Wales. *Environment and Planning A* 43, 2399–418. https://doi.org/10.1068/a43601

Crampton, J., 1995. The Ethics of GIS. *Cartography and Geographic Information Science* 22, 84–9. https://doi.org/10.1559/152304095782540546

Crow, G., Rawcliffe, S., Harris, B., 2019. Not 'Radical', but not 'Kailyard' Either: The Paisley Community Development Project Reconsidered. *Community Development Journal* 54, 501–18. https://doi.org/10.1093/cdj/bsx059

Darkes, G., Spence, M., 2017. *Cartography: An Introduction*, 2nd New edition. British Cartographic Society, London.

Datanovia, 2019. gganimate: How to Create Plots with Beautiful Animation in R. URL https://www.datanovia.com/en/blog/gganimate-how-to-create-plots-with-beautiful-animation-in-r/ (accessed 20 November 2019).

De Ingenieur, 2018. After 13 Years, Galileo Satellite Navigation Complete at Last [WWW Document]. *De Ingenieur*. URL https://www.deingenieur. nl/artikel/after-13-years-galileo-satellite-navigation-complete-at-last (accessed 4 March 2020).

Dorling, D., 1994. Cartograms for Visualizing Human Geography, in: *Visualization and GIS*. Belhaven Press, London, pp. 85–102.

Dunn, C.E., 2007. Participatory GIS — A People's GIS? *Progress in Human Geography* 31, 616–37. https://doi.org/10.1177/0309132507081493

Duporge, I., Isupova, O., Reece, S., 2019. Using Satellite Imagery and Machine Learning to Detect and Monitor Elephants [WWW Document]. *Sensing Change Blog*. URL https://blog.hexagongeospatial. com/using-satellite-imagery-and-machine-learning-to-detect-and-monitor-elephants/ (accessed 6 November 2019).

Esri, 2005. ArcGIS 9.1 Help File – Standard Classification Schemes, Natural Breaks (Jenks).

Esri, 2015. About Esri – History Up Close [WWW Document]. URL https://www.esri.com/~/media/Files/Pdfs/about-esri/esri-history-up-close (accessed 22 July 2020).

Esri, 2019. History of GIS | Early History and the Future of GIS – Esri [WWW Document]. URL https://www.esri.com/en-us/what-is-gis/h istory-of-gis (accessed 22 November 2019).

Faber, I., 2018. Animating Your Data Visualizations Like a Boss Using R [WWW Document]. *Medium*. URL https://towardsdatascience.com/ animating-your-data-visualizations-like-a-boss-using-r-f94ae20843e3 (accessed 20 November 2019).

Field, K., 2015. Cartonerd: Helecxagon Mapping. *Cartonerd*. URL http://cartonerd.blogspot.com/2015/05/helecxagon-mapping.html (accessed 21 April 2020).

Fisher, P.F., 1993. Algorithm and Implementation Uncertainty in Viewshed Analysis. *International Journal of Geographical Information Science* 7, 331–47. https://doi.org/10.1080/02693799308901965

Foley, R., Kearns, R., Kistemann, T., Wheeler, B., 2019. *Blue Space, Health and Wellbeing: Hydrophilia Unbounded*. Routledge, Abingdon.

Gilliom, J., Monahan, T., 2012. *SuperVision: An Introduction to the Surveillance Society*. University of Chicago Press, Chicago.

Gong, H., Chen, C., Bialostozky, E., Lawson, C.T., 2012. A GPS/GIS Method for Travel Mode Detection in New York City. *Computers, Environment and Urban Systems*, Special Issue: Geoinformatics 2010 36, 131–9. https://doi.org/10.1016/j.compenvurbsys.2011.05.003

Graser, A., 2018. *Learning QGIS: Create Great Maps and Perform Geoprocessing Tasks with Ease*, 4th Edition. Packt Publishing, Birmingham, UK.

Haklay, M., 2010. How Good is Volunteered Geographical Information? A Comparative Study of OpenStreetMap and Ordnance Survey Datasets. *Environment and Planning B: Urban Analytics and City Science* 37, 682–703. https://doi.org/10.1068/b35097

Haklay, M., 2013. Citizen Science and Volunteered Geographic Information: Overview and Typology of Participation, in: *Crowdsourcing Geographic Knowledge: Volunteered Geographic Information (VGI) in Theory and Practice*. London: Springer.

Hammett, D., Twyman, C., Graham, M., 2014. *Research and Fieldwork in Development*. Routledge, Milton Park, Abingdon, Oxon; New York.

Harrower, M., Brewer, C., 2003. ColorBrewer.org: An Online Tool for Selecting Colour Schemes for Maps. *The Cartographic Journal* 40, 27–37. https://doi.org/10.1179/000870403235002042

Healey, R.L., Ribchester, C., 2019. Pedagogies for Developing Undergraduate Ethical Thinking within Geography, in: *Handbook for Teaching and Learning in Geography*. Cheltenham, UK.

Hern, A., 2019. Google Fined Record £44m by French Data Protection Watchdog. *The Guardian*.

Hill, K., 2012. How Target Figured Out A Teen Girl Was Pregnant Before Her Father Did [WWW Document]. *Forbes*. URL https://www.forbes.com/sites/kashmirhill/2012/02/16/how-target-figured-out-a-teen-girl-was-pregnant-before-her-father-did/ (accessed 26 February 2020).

History of Python, 2019. Wikipedia.

Jenks, G.F., 1967. The Data Model Concept in Statistical Mapping. *International Yearbook of Cartography* 7, 186–90.

Johnson, D.E.W., 2019. Russian Election Interference and Race-Baiting. *Columbia Journal of Race and Law* 9, 191.

Laufs, J., Borrion, H., Bradford, B., 2020. Security and the Smart City: A Systematic Review. *Sustainable Cities and Society* 55, 102023. https://doi.org/10.1016/j.scs.2020.102023

Ligue des Bibliothèques Europeènnes de Recherche, 2003. National Progress Report of Great-Britain 2000–2002 [WWW Document]. URL https://web.archive.org/web/20110716212205/http://liber-maps.kb.nl/progress/20002002/uk13.html (accessed 6 November 2019).

Longley, P., Goodchild, M., Maguire, D.J., Rhind, D.W., 2010. *Geographic Information Systems and Science*. John Wiley & Sons.

Lucas, K., Wee, B. van, Maat, K., 2015. A Method to Evaluate Equitable Accessibility: Combining Ethical Theories and Accessibility-Based Approaches. *Transportation* 1–18. https://doi.org/10.1007/s11116-015-9585-2

Luebbering, C.R., 2013. Displaying the Geography of Language: The Cartography of Language Maps. *The Linguistics Journal*, 39–67.

MacEachren, A.M., 1994. Introduction to Advances in Visualizing Spatial Data, in: *Visualisation in Geographical Information Systems*. London: Belhaven Press, 51–9

Martin, D., 1992. Postcodes and the 1991 Census of Population: Issues, Problems and Prospects. *Transactions of the Institute of British Geographers* 17, 350–7.

Martin, D., 2004. Neighbourhoods and Area Statistics in the Post 2001 Census Era. *Area* 36, 136–45.

Martin, D., Nolan, A., Tranmer, M., 2001. The Application of Zone-design Methodology in the 2001 UK Census. *Environment and Planning A* 33, 1949–62. https://doi.org/10.1068/a3497

Milbert, D.G., 2000. GPS.gov: Data From the First Week Without Selective Availability [WWW Document]. https://www.gps.gov/systems/gps/modernization/sa/data/ (accessed 13 November 2019).

Minghini, M., Frassinelli, F., 2019. OpenStreetMap History for Intrinsic Quality Assessment: Is OSM Up-To-Date? *Open Geospatial Data, Software and Standards* 4, 9. https://doi.org/10.1186/s40965-019-0067-x

Ministry of Housing, Communities & Local Government, 2010. Public Sector Mapping Agreement for England and Wales: Transition Plan August 2010 [WWW Document]. *GOV.UK*. URL https://www.gov.uk/government/publications/public-sector-mapping-agreement-for-england-and-wales-transition-plan-august-2010 (accessed 6 November 2019).

National Coordination Office for Space-Based Positioning, Navigation, and Timing, 2007. GPS.gov: Selective Availability [WWW Document]. URL https://www.gps.gov/systems/gps/modernization/sa/ (accessed 13 November 2019).

Naude, J.J., Joubert, D., 2019. The Aerial Elephant Dataset: A New Public Benchmark for Aerial Object Detection. CVPR Workshop.

Newman, M., 2016. Election Maps [WWW Document]. Maps of the 2016 US Presidential Election Results. URL http://www-personal.umich.edu/~mejn/election/2016/ (accessed 21 April 2020).

Nur, K., Feng, S., Ling, C., Ochieng, W., 2013. Integration of GPS with a WiFi High Accuracy Ranging Functionality. *Geo-spatial Information Science* 16, 155–68. https://doi.org/10.1080/10095020.2013.81 7106

Openshaw, S., 1984a. Ecological Fallacies and the Analysis of Areal Census Data. *Environment and Planning A* 16, 17–31. https://doi.org/10.1068/a160017

Openshaw, S., 1984b. *The Modifiable Areal Unit Problem, CATMOG:38.* Geo Books, Norwich.

Openshaw, S., Taylor, P.J., 1981. The Modifiable Areal Unit Problem, in: *Quantitative Geography: A British View.* Routledge & Kegan Paul, London, pp. 60–9.

OpenStreetMap, 2019. OpenStreetMap [WWW Document]. About OpenStreetMap. URL https://www.openstreetmap.org/about (accessed 6 November 2019).

Ordnance Survey, 2019a. About Us | Our History [WWW Document]. URL https://www.ordnancesurvey.co.uk/about/history (accessed 6 November 2019).

Ordnance Survey, 2019b. Opening Up OS MasterMap Data [WWW Document]. URL https://www.ordnancesurvey.co.uk/business-gov ernment/tools-support/open-mastermap-programme (accessed 6 November 2019).

Phelan, D., 2019. Amazon Admits Listening To Alexa Conversations: Why It Matters [WWW Document]. *Forbes.* URL https://www. forbes.com/sites/davidphelan/2019/04/12/amazon-confirms-staff-listen-to-alexa-conversations-heres-all-you-need-to-know/ (accessed 26 February 2020).

QGIS, 2019. Wikipedia. https://en.wikipedia.org/wiki/QGIS (accessed 22 July 2020).

Riddlesden, D., Singleton, A.D., 2014. Broadband Speed Equity: A New Digital Divide? *Applied Geography* 52, 25–33. https://doi.org/10.1016/j.apgeog.2014.04.008

Riggs, P.D., Dean, D.J., 2007. An Investigation into the Causes of Errors and Inconsistencies in Predicted Viewsheds. *Transactions in GIS* 11, 175–96. https://doi.org/10.1111/j.1467-9671.2007.01040.x

RStudio, 2019. About RStudio [WWW Document]. URL https://rstudio.com/about/ (accessed 22 November 2019).

Ruane, E., Birhane, A., Ventresque, A., 2019. *Conversational AI: Social and Ethical Considerations*. Conference: AICS - 27th AIAI Irish Conference on Artificial Intelligence and Cognitive Science, At Galway, Ireland.

Scull, P., Burnett, A., Dolfi, E., Goldfarb, A., Baum, P., 2016. Privacy and Ethics in Undergraduate GIS Curricula. *Journal of Geography* 115, 24–34. https://doi.org/10.1080/00221341.2015.1017517

Shulevitz, S. 2018. Alexa, Should We Trust You? *The Atlantic*. https://www.theatlantic.com/magazine/archive/2018/11/alexa-how-will-you-change-us/570844/ (accessed 26 February 2020).

Singleton, A.D., 2014. Why Geographers Should Learn to Code. *Geographical Magazine, Royal Geographical Society* (with the IBG) 77.

Singleton, A.D., Dolega, L., Riddlesden, D., Longley, P.A., 2016. Measuring the Spatial Vulnerability of Retail Centres to Online Consumption through a Framework of E-resilience. *Geoforum* 69, 5–18. https://doi.org/10.1016/j.geoforum.2015.11.013

Stevens, M., Vitos, M., Altenbuchner, J., Conquest, G., Lewis, J., Haklay, M., 2014. Taking Participatory Citizen Science to Extremes. *IEEE Pervasive Computing* 13, 20–9. https://doi.org/10.1109/MPRV.2014.37

The Big Mac index, 2019. The Economist.

Thieme, N., 2018. R generation. *Significance* 15, 14–19. https://doi.org/10.1111/j.1740-9713.2018.01169.x

Tomlinson, R.F., 1966. A Geographic Information System for Regional Planning, in: Stewart, G.A. (Ed.), *Land Evaluation*. Macmillian, Melbourne, pp. 200–10.

Van Sickle, J., 2015. *GPS for Land Surveyors*, Fourth edition. CRC Press, Taylor & Francis Group, Boca Raton.

Wang, D., Shao, Q., Yue, H., 2019. Surveying Wild Animals from Satellites, Manned Aircraft and Unmanned Aerial Systems (UASs): A Review. *Remote Sensing* 11, 1308. https://doi.org/10.3390/rs11111308

Wheeler, B.W., Cooper, A.R., Page, A.S., Jago, R., 2010. Greenspace and Children's Physical Activity: A GPS/GIS Analysis of the PEACH Project. *Preventive Medicine* 51, 148–52. https://doi.org/10.1016/j.ypmed.2010.06.001

White, M.P., Pahl, S., Wheeler, B.W., Fleming, L.E.F., Depledge, M.H., 2016. The 'Blue Gym': What Can Blue Space Do For You and

What Can You Do For Blue Space? *Journal of the Marine Biological Association of the United Kingdom* 96, 5–12. https://doi.org/10.1017/S0025315415002209

Wikipedia, 2019. History of OpenStreetMap – OpenStreetMap Wiki [WWW Document]. URL https://wiki.openstreetmap.org/wiki/History_of_OpenStreetMap (accessed 6 November 2019).

Yuan, M., 2017. 30 Years of IJGIS: The Changing Landscape of Geographical Information Science and the Road Ahead. *International Journal of Geographical Information Science* 31, 425–34. https://doi.org/10.1080/13658816.2016.1236928

Index

Figures in italics